KV-031-475

FOODS FOR HEALTH

James Hewitt was born in Belfast, where he was a reporter
for a Fleet Street daily newspaper. On moving to London in
1963, he worked in publishing, as a research worker for the
Foreign Office, and as joint warden, with his wife, of a hostel
for blind people.

He is now a full-time freelance writer and has written
more than thirty books covering a wide range of subjects:
historical events, exploration, photography, diet, physical fitness, relaxation, Yoga and meditation. He is the author of
Yoga and *Meditation*, also published in the Teach Yourself
series.

TEACH YOURSELF BOOKS

James Hewitt

FOODS FOR HEALTH
a guide to natural nutrition

Illustrated by Heather Sherratt

TEACH YOURSELF BOOKS
Hodder and Stoughton

First printed 1981

British Library Cataloguing in Publication Data

Hewitt, James
    Food for health. – (Teach yourself books).
    1. Food, Natural
    I. Title
    641.3′02   TX369
    ISBN 0 340 26749 6

*Filmset by Northumberland Press Ltd, Gateshead, Tyne and Wear
Printed and bound in Great Britain for Hodder and Stoughton
paperbacks, a division of Hodder and Stoughton Ltd, Mill Road,
Dunton Green, Sevenoaks, Kent, (Editorial Office; 47 Bedford
Square, London, WC1B 3DP) by
Richard Clay (The Chaucer Press) Ltd,
Bungay, Suffolk*

Contents

Acknowledgements

The author and publisher wish to thank the following for permission to publish extracts from the following works: D. C. Jarvis, *Folk Medicine*, 1960, W. H. Allen & Co. Ltd, Messrs. Henry Holt & Co. Inc.; Professor M. Petkov cit. P. Dixon, *Ginseng*, 1976, G. Duckworth & Co. Ltd; D. K. Payler, *The Lancet*, 1973, Dr Munroe, Hodder & Stoughton Ltd; Peter Cleave, *The Saccharine Disease*, 1974, John Wright & Sons Ltd; Lawrence Galton, *The Truth About Fibre In Your Diet*, 1976, Crown Publishers Inc.; J. Wynne-Tyson, *Food For A Future – the Ecological Priority of a Humane Diet*, 1979, Centaur Press Ltd; Wilfrid E. Shute, *Complete Updated Vitamin E Book*, 1975, Keats Publishing Inc.; Roger Williams, *Nutrition Against Disease*, 1971, Pitman Books Ltd; Kenneth Heaton preface, Jeanne Jones, *Fabulous Fibre Cookbook*, 1978, Pitman House, Charles Scribners' Sons; Lloyd Percival, *The American Bee Journal*, 1955, Danant Publishing Inc.; James Rorty, *Bio-Organics*, 1956, Devin-Adair Inc.; Curtis Wood Jr., *Calories, Vitamins and Common Sense*, 1959, Exposition Press, 1962, Belmont Books; C. F. Leyel, *The Truth About Herbs*, 1954, Culpeper Press; Sir Arbuthnot Lane, *Prevention of Diseases Peculiar to Civilisation*; Rutherford Platt, *The Great American Forest*, 1965, Prentice-Hall Inc.

Foreword

In recent years, many people have been won over, totally or in part, by the food reformists' arguments, whose case is based mainly on a criticism of modern foodstuffs, which are said to be denatured and devitalised through the processes of refining, and to be polluted by chemicals used in agriculture and in food processing.

On the positive side, it is believed that health is attained and maintained and resistance to disease built up when the diet is based on natural whole foods, free from refining and from chemical additives. These foods have been given the name 'health foods'. Specialist shops supply them, though they are also appearing more and more in general food stores, which is proof of a growing public demand for 'safe' and health-enhancing foods.

The newcomer to health foods, who is prepared to give them a fair trial, will, I hope, appreciate this guide to what may at first seem a bewildering array of foods and food products, diet supplements, natural remedies, and so on. People already buying health foods regularly may also appreciate a survey of what is available and what they may do in promoting better health and resisting disease.

At the same time, I will be outlining the basic approach to eating for health that motivates the inclusion of health foods in the diet. This is important. For it is the essence of the food reformist's position that it is the *total diet*, which is based on wholesome natural foods, that effects changes in health, vitality, and well-being, and which protects from the 'diseases of civilisation', rather than reliance on this or that particular health food, regardless of the claims made for it.

Our concern, in short, is not any form of faddism, but natural nutrition.

James Hewitt

Why Health Foods?

In recent years, the sale of health foods has shown a rapid growth. In America, Britain, and in some European countries the number of specialist health food shops has increased by hundreds, and they now present shiny modern fronts in the High Streets and main shopping precincts. Chain stores, too, are responding to public demand by including more and more 'health foods' on their shelves, and sometimes they have special 'health foods' sections.

Food reformists recognise that ideally every food shop should be selling those foods most beneficial to health, but until public awareness grows to sufficient dimensions to make this possible, there will continue to be a need for specialist health food shops.

Why the rapid growth in the sales and consumption of health foods?

Health food stores have long catered for the requirements of food reformists, vegetarians, vegans, and advocates of natural healing. There has been an increase in the number of people who for reasons of health, ethics, aesthetics, and spiritual values have given up eating meat and become vegetarians. There has been, too, an increase in the number of people looking to diet reform as a way of preventing disease, and to natural remedies when things go wrong with health. But the main boost to the sales and consumption of health foods has come from growing public anxiety about the nature – perhaps better the *denaturing* – of foodstuffs. The loss of quality and the danger stems from the practices of modern farming and from the methods of modern food processing.

What's wrong with modern food?

The greatly increased demand for health foods is part of a reaction against the nutritional inferiority and chemical adulteration of modern food. What perturb more and more people are:

1   Pollution of the environment by noxious chemical substances which get into the air we breathe and into foods eaten by farm animals and by ourselves.
2   The use of toxic insecticides to spray crops; the use of hormones and antibiotics in rearing livestock, and some other modern farming methods.
3   The use of chemical fertilisers rather than natural organic methods of crop cultivation.
4   The denaturing and devitalising of foods through refining, which strips foods of vitamins, minerals, and other nutrients, and at the same time removes dietary fibre.
5   The use of synthetic chemical additives in food processing, for preserving, flavouring, colouring, and so on.
6   The loss of flavour and texture in modern foods resulting from these processes.

Unease over even one of these six criteria is enough to justify the purchase and consumption of health foods.

Environmental pollution

The growth of the health food trade is associated with the upsurge of concern about environmental pollution and ecology. Ecology – 'the study of the reciprocal relationships between organisms and their surroundings' – has become a familiar media word. Food contamination is part of the ecological picture.

Environmental pollution is not new. It has been a growing problem since the Industrial Revolution at the beginning of the nineteenth century, but the problem did not become serious – or at any rate was not taken seriously – until after World War II. Rapid technological advance is much to blame.

There may be danger in the air we breathe, in drinking water, and in food, whether plant or animal. Much food grown for farm animals or ourselves is contaminated by industrial waste, by lead from the exhausts of motor vehicles, by radioactivity, distributed on a global scale by the atomic testing programmes of the early 1960s and by other environmental pollutants.

'The contamination of food is the final stage of a sequence of events starting with the discharge of the agent and its subsequent movement through various levels of the environment into the food,' says Jack Lucas in his book *Our Polluted Food*. Contaminated foods cause internal body pollution and disease. However, governments have taken a lot of persuading before they will agree that the level of toxic substances in air or food is too high for health safety.

Consider briefly the following cause for concern. In many industrial areas there is a disturbing rise in the amount of lead in the air and in foodstuffs. The presence of lead in the body harms the brain and nervous tissue, particularly in young children. And if a sufficiently high percentage occurs chronic mental deterioration may result. Schools should not be built close to motorways or to places where there is continuous daily traffic of motor vehicles. Lead may also harm the red blood cells, causing anaemia. And some medical investigations suggest that lead interferes with the biochemical processes whereby enzymes release energy. There is also some evidence to show that raised lead levels are related to stillbirths.

Dr H. L. Needleman and colleagues in the US have shown that children with increased blood-lead and tooth-lead have lower than average IQs. They have also shown a relationship between high exposure to lead and behavioural problems in children. Dr Needleman's studies were of children in typical urban areas of industrial cities.

In March 1980, Professor Michael Rutter, head of the department of Child and Adolescent Psychiatry at London University's Institute of Psychiatry, wrote in a supplement to the journal

Developmental Medicine and Child Neurology that the Needleman investigation 'provides the most impressive evidence to date on the possibly damaging effects of raised lead levels in the range previously considered harmless and which are found in some twenty per cent of children in the general population'.

Lead danger comes from industrial emissions, from lead piping carrying domestic water supplies, and from the fumes from the exhausts of motor traffic: but most lead gets into the body through contaminated food.

Toxic insecticides

The use of poisonous pesticides greatly increased after World War II. Food reformists warn that pesticide residues have become part of the human diet. It is now difficult to buy fruits and vegetables which have not been sprayed with insecticides. You should wash fruits and vegetables well before eating to reduce the amount of possible toxic residue; some people may also wish to peel fruits, even though this entails a loss of vitamins which are concentrated in the peel or skin.

According to food reformists, there is a further danger in modern farming. Rapid growth of farm animals and poultry is promoted by the use of hormones, the residues of which are present in the meat and poultry flesh people eat. Antibiotic residues to control diseases in livestock may also be present. Modern factory farming methods are also believed to lower the nutritional value of foods, and certainly reduce their taste.

Governmental health safety bodies assert that the level of toxics in food are not so high as to cause concern; but they have been known to change their minds after years of allowing the use of a chemical. Action was not taken against the use of the insecticide DDT, a nerve poison, until after years of campaigning by people who recognised the danger.

Benefits derived from the use of man-made chemicals have to be weighed against the associated risks and the harm done. There have been the dramatic and unmistakable tragedies, such as the horrendous effects of the defoliant 'Agent Orange' used by the Americans to strip jungle cover in Vietnam in 1962 and of the explosion at a chemical works at Seveso, Italy, in 1976. In both these cases, and elsewhere, the damage to human health and destruction of life – chloracne, abortions, birth defects, and cancer – were due to the presence of dioxin, a poison so deadly that a few specks of it can kill. Yet dioxin is only a useless by-product of the manufacture of herbicides.

A BBC programme about dioxin, screened in March 1980, spoke of 'a chemical tidal wave – from America 40,000 pesticides alone. Pesticides, herbicides, fungicides, bactericides – all designed to kill some specific target. But some chemicals are not designed at all. They just occur – invisible, potent, little understood and useless by-products which nobody wants. The most deadly of these is called dioxin'.

Dramatic accidents only highlight the risks; the long-term effects of pesticides and other killer chemicals absorbed through the diet have not been adequately investigated, and food reformists today are convinced they are pointing to dangers that will be recognised by medical scientists in future years.

Organic farming

Food reformists oppose the use of artificial fertilisers and favour the organic method of growing food, using compost. Though chemical fertilisers may make plants grow rapidly and to large size, food reformists are convinced that food grown organically contains more nutritional value. They cite scientific studies which support this view. They say that foods grown organically also taste better, and that plants grown in humus or compost are very resistant to disease, as are animals fed on such plants. But perhaps the main plank of the case against artificial fertilisers is that eventually, because of their use, the soil deteriorates, loses its minerals, and ceases to be 'living soil'.

Humus is made up of organic matter, such as plant residues and animal droppings, which bacteria process into food for the plants. In the organic system, when a crop is removed humus is prepared in the form of compost and spread over the ground to give life back to the soil.

Compost, whether for fields or garden, can be made from anything that was once living – weeds, leaves, grass cuttings, animal and bird dung, fruit and vegetable peelings, tea leaves, egg shells, even paper. Humus and compost are dense with beneficial bacteria.

Artificial fertilisers deplete the soil's population of earthworms.

Rich soil contains as many as 1,750,000 earthworms per acre. This helps the farmer in two ways:

1   They chew and digest organic matter, then pass it out as casts that are a superb form of humus.
2   They make 'tunnels' in the soil which allow the soil to breathe and to store water.

The pioneer work of Sir Albert Howard led to the setting up of the Soil Association in Britain in 1946. His experiences in India made him a leading campaigner for the organic farming system. In 1905 he became Economic Botanist to the Agricultural Institute set up by Lord Curzon at Pusa in Bengal. At Indore, he experimented with making compost, and his method is still known as the 'Indore method'. He observed that when 'everything went back into the land' crops and animals which fed on the crops were resistant to disease, whereas both crops and livestock raised on farms using artificial fertilisers had lower resistance to disease. He deliberately put his healthy oxen on land on which diseased cattle had grazed and also allowed his oxen to have direct contact by rubbing noses with animals which had foot-and-mouth disease.

'Nothing happened,' he reported. 'The healthy, well-fed animals reacted to this disease exactly as suitable varieties of crops, when properly grown, do to insect and fungus pests – no infection took place. Nor did any infection occur as the result of my oxen using common pastures. This experience was repeated year after year between 1910 and 1923, when I left Pusa for Indore.'

'Natural farming' can be successful. Mr S. Myall, Vice-President of the Soil Association in Britain, turned his 600-acre farm over to organic methods and in eleven years increased his output to above the national average per acre. Moreover, the quality of his crops and the robustness of his livestock were improved.

Artificial fertilisers are convenient and in some cases produce large plants. But bigger is not necessarily better. Studies in Britain have shown that grain grown with farmyard manure contains more Vitamin B than that grown with artificial fertiliser. Other studies could be cited supporting the food reformist's belief that organically grown food is of unsurpassed nutritional quality.

Food refining

The average diet of the people of the world's most affluent nations is high in calories, yet low in nourishment – producing the seeming paradox of millions of people both over-fed, and at the same time under-nourished. Health foodists – if I may be allowed that term – consider that refining foods is mainly responsible for this nutritional deficiency. And health foods are a reaction to this situation.

A high intake of calories is responsible for overweight and obesity, and for disease. Refining, canning, and other modern processing methods rob foods of their minerals, vitamins, and other nutrients. The worst example of this is white sugar, the consumption of which has grown enormously in the last hundred years. It supplies energy, and nothing more. The raw sugar cane has been denuded of its minerals and vitamins. Tooth decay, starting in young children, is just one harmful aspect of the high consumption of sugar. Obesity is another. A build up of fat in the body causes diseases of the cardio-vascular system. Sugar is very high in calories, yet in its refined form contributes nothing useful in the way of nutrients essential to health, and the energy it supplies can be easily obtained from other foods.

The application of technology to food production developed in the nineteenth century to meet the needs of the great numbers of people who moved from rural to urban areas, so cutting themselves off from local food cultivation and preparation. In the early years of the Industrial Revolution, there was a rapid increase in the number of bakeries and in the manufacture of bread, biscuits, cakes, jams, and confectionery. Before, bread was traditionally baked at home, using barley, rye and oats. It was brown, firm-textured, packed with nutrients, and had lots of fibre. The new bakeries used wheat and soon catered for a preference for white bread and for white flour products. More food was imported to feed the great urban populations. After about 1850, there was also a rapid growth in the consumption of sugar.

Food reformists are strongly against 'the four whites': white sugar, white flour and its products, white rice, and common salt. In their eyes, the refined carbohydrate foods – like white sugar, bread, and rice – supply 'empty calories'. The natural cereals and the sugar cane have been denatured and devitalised. These 'empty' foods supply energy, but nothing or little more. They put on weight because they are high in calorific content, fail to satisfy the appetite, so encouraging over-consumption, and they are addictive. They fool the body's appetite regulator: the person hooked on the concentrated carbohydrate foods goes on eating more and more and does not know when to stop. The person with a 'sweet tooth' piles up calories out of all proportion to the amount of energy expended. The result is a dangerous build up of fat in the body. In contrast, health foods are strong in flavour and in bulk and so satisfy the appetite, making them difficult to overeat.

The bulk in health foods is supplied by dietary fibre, which is low in the refined foods. You will not go short of dietary fibre if you regularly eat plenty of vegetables, fruits, nuts, whole grains, wholewheat bread, bran, and wheat germ. Indigestible fibre – inaccurately called roughage – promotes the movement of food in the alimentary tract. With a refined diet, the movement is slow; with a high-fibre diet, it speeds up greatly. Food reformists believe the inclusion of plenty of fibre in the diet prevents diseases such as diverticulitis and cancer of the bowel. Many doctors now support this view. Such diseases are rare among people whose diet is high in fibre. Their stools are bulky and moist. Speeding up the movement of food in the bowel increases the likelihood of contaminating agents being expelled with the faeces. We will discuss the importance of dietary fibre more fully in Chapter 5.

Chemical additives

A fourth problem with the modern diet is that the great majority of commercial foods contain synthetic chemicals. These are added during processing, for reasons of mass appeal (colour, flavour, texture), mass distribution (and the need for long shelf life), and maximum profitability. Public concern about external pollution is matched by disquiet over possible internal pollution through contaminated foods.

The use of chemical additives began in the nineteenth century, to meet the need for feeding the growing city populations but also to increase profit. Additives were often used to mask deterioration of food or 'pad out' foods with cheaper substances. Public health was endangered by these practices. In Britain, the Food and Drugs Act, 1860, was introduced so that there could be some control over the quality of food provided to the public. At first only a few chemicals were used, but their use has increased rapidly in the present century, along with advances in food technology. Today more than three thousand chemicals are available for use in food processing – for preserving, flavouring, colouring, stabilising, emulsifying, and so on. They 'improve' appearance, texture, and palatability. Food reformists believe that their use is unnecessary in most cases and that some commonly used chemicals are very harmful to health in the long term.

It is not claimed that all additives are harmful. The majority may well be innocuous. At least two additives could even be classified themselves as health foods. They are agar-agar, which comes from seaweeds and is often used as a stabiliser, and lecithin, which is used as an emulsifier in soft margarines, ice cream, etc. But over some chemical additives a question mark must hang. The problem for the consumer is that it is difficult to determine which chemical additives are safe and which are doubtful.

Testing the safety of chemical additives is a complex scientific task. The story so far of their investigation does not inspire confidence. The cautious report 'no *apparent* adverse effect' is often used. How do you accurately measure the possible harm done to the health of human beings by individual chemicals and combinations of chemicals over a period of twenty years, which some studies indicate is often the time which goes by before the symptoms of damage become observable? The customary method of testing is to give massive doses of a chemical to laboratory animals. Tests with laboratory animals can be an unreliable guide to what effect a substance has on people. Animals tested with thalidomide produced *no* malformation in their offspring, and penicillin – a human lifesaver – even in minute quantities kills guinea pigs!

It can take many years for a government to decide that a food additive could harm human health and to ban it. For example, agene, which was used in making white bread, was banned in Britain after thirty years of campaigning by food reformists. Its successor, chlorine dioxide, has been the subject of persistent attacks. Another additive in bread in the UK – potassium bromate – is banned in South Africa. Synthetic anti-oxidants were banned, then reinstated, and then allowed in limited quantities in certain foods. According to British newspaper reports, white bread contains up to twenty chemical additives. Only five colouring additives are permitted in the USA, but the British government allows twenty-four to be used.

Doubt about the safety of chemical additives, together with fears about pesticide and other residues in food, is probably more responsible than anything else for so many people turning to additive-free health foods.

Food reformists campaigned for many years for the contents of commercial foods to be detailed on their labels. If you are uneasy about chemical additives, then you should read the labels. It is depressing to find that only a small minority of the packaged and tinned foods on general sale are free from synthetic flavourings, colourings, preservatives, or some other 'improvers'. Total avoidance of foods containing artificial chemical additives is the stoic response of the dedicated. How far you follow their example is for you to decide. If you base your diet strongly on additive-free health foods, and otherwise look after your body with adequate exercise, fresh air, and relaxation, you will probably be able to cope with any small amounts of questionable chemicals that are in a little of the food you eat. I mention this, as total abstention from foods containing additives requires diligence and dedication. Most – though not always all – foods sold in health food shops are free of synthetic chemicals.

Loss of flavour and texture

There is a final factor to be considered in discussing what the food reformist and health foodist find wrong with food today. That is the blandness and diminution of natural flavour. A desire to know the real flavour of foods would be justification in itself for eating more natural whole foods and patronising your nearest health food store. Organically grown vegetables, cereals, and fruits taste better than those forced with artificial fertilisers. Studies have shown that they are also superior nutritionally. Eggs laid by free-range hens taste better than those produced by the battery system, and free-range poultry meats taste better too.

A generation is growing up which knows only a bland uniformity of flavour in foods. Older people recall nostalgically how food used to taste. This can only partly be accounted for by a natural decrease in taste response or a trick of memory ('We used to have lovely hot summers!') Smoking muffles taste response, so that only the spiciest foods 'get through' to the heavy smoker's deadened taste buds.

Compared with wholewheat bread, with its nutty flavour and crisp, firm texture, white bread is bland and textureless, an apology for real bread. Refined white sugar offers no smell and a sweetness that does not satisfy but nevertheless triggers a craving for more.

The ultimate answer to the adulteration of taste, texture, and aroma of foods through refining, processing, and technological farming is to grow your own vegetables and fruit, to keep your own poultry and perhaps a goat, to bake your own bread, and so on. For those for whom this is impossible – city and flat-dwellers – purchase organically grown food and natural whole foods from suppliers of health foods.

'The diseases of civilisation'

'More people are living longer. The number of old people is becoming a serious social problem in many areas. So there can't be much, if anything, wrong with the modern diet.' This is a frequently heard rejoinder to the food reformists' criticisms of refined and adulterated foods and the call for a return to whole foods. This argument overlooks several factors, not least the present epidemic of degenerative diseases, sometimes called 'the diseases of civilisation'.

Modern hygiene, drugs, and surgery keep more people alive into old age, though their level of health and fitness is mostly nothing to celebrate. People are not to any notable extent living to very advanced ages – not any more than did the survivors of the infectious diseases in earlier centuries. Centenarians, fit or unfit, are still an oddity. And doctors have been puzzled and alarmed by the rapid growth of heart disease, cancer, diabetes, and other killers.

The term 'diseases of civilisation' refers to various degenerative diseases which have increased dramatically during the present century in affluent countries, but are rare or unknown in primitive societies. Twentieth-century medicine and improved methods of hygiene now control many infectious diseases such as influenza, diphtheria, and tuberculosis, which used to kill thousands of men, women, and children each year. But the degenerative, non-infectious diseases have risen to epidemic proportions, despite huge sums of money being spent on medical research. An alarming feature of this epidemic is that the diseases are appearing more frequently in younger people.

In the affluent, Western countries, coronary heart disease is the Number One killer; yet it was not a common health problem one hundred years ago. Next is cancer, followed by diabetes, which was only twenty-seventh in the 'killer table' in 1900. Other 'diseases of civilisation' are hypertension (high blood pressure), narrowing of the arteries, stomach ulcers, obesity, constipation, diverticulitis, intestinal complaints, migraine, tooth decay (dental caries), hepatitis, disseminated sclerosis, insomnia, and a range of mental illnesses.

Why the increase in the diseases and disorders of twentieth-century civilisation?

The medical experts and researchers have their theories and their controversies. Those include: inadequate exercise and stress; faults in choice of diet (it is now widely believed, though not conclusively proved, that saturated animal fats cause a build up of excessive cholesterol in the blood, leading to narrowing of the arteries and some eminent doctors and nutritionists link the high consumption of refined sugar with several of the diseases listed above).

Food reformists believe that these diseases are primarily caused by a deterioration in the quality of the foods people eat and the addition to them of harmful chemicals. They point to the fact that these diseases increase proportionately with higher consumption of refined foods and the use of synthetic chemicals in processing. They point, too, to how people living in primitive or isolated societies are free from these diseases, yet start contracting them if introduced to the typical Western diet. There is often a period of about twenty years before the symptoms of the diseases are observed. This fits in with the food reformist's views that the modern refined diet is a form of slow poisoning.

A powerful attack on the refined concentrated carbohydrate foods, in particular on white sugar and white flour, is mounted by Cleave, Campbell, and Painter in *The Saccharine Disease*. The title of their book has nothing to do with the artificial sweetener of that name: the authors use the word 'saccharine' to mean 'related to sugar'. They say that white sugar and white flour and its products are highly concentrated carbohydrates, lacking in fibre, which it is all too easy to over-eat. This over-consumption is responsible for the epidemic of coronary heart disease, hypertension, diabetes, and other diseases and disorders. The connection between over-consumption of refined carbohydrates and obesity is clear, as is that between obesity and putting a strain on the heart and other body organs.

The removal of fibre in refining comes in for particularly strong attack. Refined flour and sugar cause tooth decay (dental caries), another disease of civilisation. Moistened white flour sticks to the teeth. Plaque, a sticky film, forms on the teeth and gums. Bacteria feed and breed in the plaque and release acids which cause tooth decay and gum disease. The damage from refined sugar is even more rapid.

A more serious problem resulting from lack of dietary fibre is that food residues move very slowly through the large intestine. Diverticulitis now afflicts one-third of all people over sixty. The pressure of excess food residue causes bulges in the muscular wall of the intestine, which may produce infection and peritonitis. Deaths from this cause have increased greatly.

A further objection to the refined carbohydrates by the authors of *The Saccharine Disease* is that the protein content of the whole food is greatly reduced in refining. Protein is necessary, they say, to buffer the gastric juices and to protect the mucous lining of the stomach. Without sufficient protein, the gastric juices attack the lining of the stomach and cause ulcers. Eating protein foods with refined carbohydrate does not provide proper protection.

Doctors Cleave, Campbell, and Painter give a mass of evidence to support their views on the damage done to health by the refined carbohydrate foods.

Malnutrition and affluence

We still sometimes read or hear the orthodox medical viewpoint: 'The average British or European or American diet contains all the nutrients necessary for good health.' But more and more doctors are voicing a different opinion. It is now widely recognised that it is possible to be over-fed (in terms of energy units, i.e. calories) and yet to be under-nourished (in terms of nutritional elements). Income has nothing to do with it. A millionaire's family may be poorly fed, missing out on essential vitamins and minerals.

Medical research and food reformist opinion have come closer in recent years, and indeed overlap significantly in places. Those doctors who see the need for more emphasis on prevention of disease rather than on treating symptoms are recognising that sound and balanced nutrition, based on safe wholesome foods, is the prime requirement.

In 1972, Dr George M. Briggs of the University of California, told the Senate Committee on Nutrition and Human Needs: 'Americans have turned into a nation of nutritional illiterates who know so little about what to eat that the annual cost of malnutrition among rich and poor alike may be $30 billion . . . The development of fabricated foods containing nothing but calories is irresponsible.'

In the same year Dr Roger J. Williams of the University of Texas, who discovered panthothenic acid and the man who gave folic acid its name, reported as a member of President Nixon's Advisory Panel on Heart Disease:

'The sins of omission occasioned by modern industrialisation of food production without adequate regard for nutritional value are many. Among the essential nutrient items likely to be deficient or out of balance in the supermarket produce commonly consumed are Vitamin B6, magnesium, Vitamin E, Vitamin C, folic acid and trace minerals. This is not a complete list, but these items all appear to be involved in the heart disease problem. All these and other nutrient items are needed to keep the cells and tissues of hearts and blood vessels healthy.

Mental retardation, dental disease, arthritis, mental disease, alcoholism and possibly even cancer, can be blamed on poor internal environments which the cells and tissues of our bodies have to live with. These environments can be vastly improved by nutritional means . . .

In a 1971 two-volume report issued by the US Department of Agriculture, it is estimated that in the case of thirteen common, serious diseases, twenty per cent to ninety per cent relief can be looked for as a result of nutritional research.'

Can it really be true that the majority of people belonging to the richest and most powerful nation in the world are suffering from malnutrition, without most of them knowing it? An American doctor and a lay expert on nutrition say that it is true. James Rorty and Dr N. Philip Norman write in *Bio-organics: Your Food and Your Health*:

> 'Even if we were to end poverty in America, we would not thereby end malnutrition. We have also to correct our perverted food habits, and underlying these, the distorted pattern of food production, food processing, and food distribution which developed during the Age of Nutritional Innocence, and which are by no means easy to change.'

Wartime health

Strangely, as has often been pointed out, people's health in Britain and other European countries improved during World War II and for the few years of food rationing that followed the end of the war; in many respects it was better than it is today, despite today's much higher standard of living. The economic and other realities of war forced people to eat less sugar and a loaf high in whole wheat.

The improved health of the British people then amazed many people. But it did not surprise the doctors, nutritionists, and biochemists who advised the government at that time. Certainly it was no surprise to the 600 'panel' health-insurance doctors in Cheshire who had taken part in a remarkable experiment just before the war. Their representative committee had issued a 'Medical Testament' on 22 March 1939. While acknowledging the improvement in medical care and in life expectancy resulting from the operation of the National Health Insurance Act during twenty-five years, they pointed out that much remained to be done if its stated purpose – 'the prevention and cure of sickness' – was to be fulfilled. There was a great improvement in cure – but what about *prevention*? 'On the first and major count (prevention) the Act has done nothing,' they reported. 'We feel that the fact should be faced. Our daily work brings us repeatedly to the same point: "*This illness results from a lifetime of wrong nutrition.*"'

The Cheshire doctors did something about the problem they delineated. Less illness in the county meant less work for the doctors. They were paid so much annually per 'panel' patient registered with them, and this remained a fixed payment regardless of the amount of illness being treated. The 600 doctors thus had an incentive in trying to prevent diseases and disorders among their patients. The 'testament' reported how successful they were. They concentrated on the one factor they could influence and which they believed was most important – 'wrong nutrition'.

They instructed village bakers in the baking of loaves using freshly-ground wholewheat flour, half of its weight being raw wheat germ with its rich store of minerals, vitamins, and enzymes. The wheat itself was grown by the organic 'Indore method' mentioned earlier. The villagers were encouraged to eat whole-wheat bread, oatmeal porridge, raw milk, cheese, eggs, green leafy vegetables, abundant salads, a moderate but regular amount of meat, with liver weekly, fish, potatoes baked or boiled in their skins, and plenty of fresh fruit.

There is not the space here to report in detail on the success of this experiment. Marked success was achieved in improving the health of children. Pregnant women who followed the diet des-cribed above nearly always produced healthy children.

'The children are splendid,' the Cheshire doctors reported. 'As infants they sleep as well as could be wished, grow well, are not over-fat but weigh well and very seldom "ail anything". Broncho-pneumonia, for example, is almost unknown among them. One of their most striking features is their good humour and happiness. They are sturdy limbed, beautifully skinned, normal children . . .'

In short, in Cheshire in the years before World War II, when relative incomes were much lower than they are today, an enter-prising group of doctors effected a valuable transformation in the health of their patients by putting them on a wholesome diet based on natural whole foods – a diet which we now associate with the description 'health foods'.

During the war years that followed, sugar supplies were rationed and the British government introduced the National Wholemeal Loaf. The people's health improved, as had the health of the Cheshire villagers a few years before. Unfortunately, once rationing ended, most British people slipped back into over-consumption of the nutritionally 'empty' refined sugars and starches. When sweets were de-rationed in the early 1950s, there was a mad rush that cleared the shops of stocks and rationing had for a time to be reintroduced. Today the United Kingdom's *per capita* consumption of confectionery, biscuits and cakes is one of the highest in the world. One outcome is the shockingly high incidence of tooth decay, starting in children. Two-thirds of British adults are toothless by the age of forty-five.

What are health foods?

The main planks of the food reformist's argument are given above and, the essential nature of what constitutes health foods should now be clear.

He will

– turn to foods which are organically grown and free from pesticide and other residues resulting from forced-growth farming, whether of plant or flesh.
– turn to foods free from synthetic chemical additives, to foods which have not been added to or adulterated. Hundreds, even thousands, of these additives may be taken into the body every week, and the effect of the accumulation of chemicals in the bloodstream is likely to be harmful to health, perhaps seriously so.
– turn to natural whole foods which have not been stripped of their nutrients either wholly or partially through the processes of refining.
– turn to foods that retain plenty of dietary fibre, which keep food moving smoothly through the intestines.
– turn to foods which retain the texture and taste of 'real' foods which have been neither denatured nor devitalised.

Recognising the dangerous depletion of minerals, vitamins, and other nutrients in so much of today's diet and the importance of taking all the nutrients regularly in balanced amounts, he will probably make use of some of the natural food supplements, thereby avoiding any nutritional deficiencies.

In short, he or she will turn to *health foods*.

Health foods reflect and supply the needs of people who believe that many of the foods eaten today are toxic, or possibly toxic, and nutritionally depleted by modern methods of food growing and processing.

The term 'health foods' may be criticised, though it is not a misnomer like 'slimming foods' (no foods take off weight!). Some people prefer to use the terms 'whole foods' and 'natural foods', though it is possible to pick holes in these terms also. Even the keenest health-foodist does not eat the shell of a nut or the skin of a banana. While what is 'natural' or 'unnatural' has always been tricky semantic territory. Not all of nature's plants are health foods – some could kill you or make you very ill. Primitive man learned what diet was good for him by trial and error, and in the early stages there must have been some painful lessons to learn. But allowing that the terms health foods, whole foods, and natural foods have their weaknesses, they still point clearly enough to a certain choice of diet and to certain qualities of food.

Common foods, familiar for many centuries, such as bread, milk, cheese, breakfast cereals, vegetables, and fruit, are – or rather should be – health foods. Newcomers to shopping for health foods may be forgiven for feeling something of what Molière's M. Jourdain felt (in *Le Bourgeois Gentilhomme*) on discovering that he had been talking prose for the last forty years and had never known it. Many health foods are foods familiar to most people from childhood. But there *are* important differences, which will be described when I come to discuss specific health foods in the chapters that follow.

The differences between health foods and their counterparts on sale from supermarkets can be understood in a general way from the description of what constitutes the essential nature of health foods given above. The differences are important to the health-foodist, who is prepared to pay a little extra for what is believed to be foods superior in nutrition, taste, and protection against disease. Mass-produced and mass-distributed foods are bound to be cheaper than those handled by the health food trade, which makes up, despite its rapid growth, only a small percentage of the total food trade.

Common foods are only part of what is on sale in the health food store. Whole foods probably take up only about one-third of the shelf space. Convenience foods are gaining ground: but they make use of natural ingredients and are normally free from synthetic chemical additives. Health food shops also sell dietary supplements – brewer's yeast, molasses, wheat germ, bran, kelp tablets, and so on. Natural sources of the important vitamins and minerals are available. There are special 'snacks', based often on dried fruits, seeds, nuts, carob, etc. Natural cosmetics is a growing line. Herbs and natural preparations for treating illnesses and bodily discomforts have always been part of the health food trade. This is natural in a movement which believes that good food is the best medicine and that we should co-operate as much as possible with nature both in diet and in healing.

Belief in food reform and in natural healing are not necessarily the same thing, but they often coincide or overlap to some extent.

Some health food stores sell fresh fruits and vegetables that have been grown organically and are free from pesticide residues. The few health food shops that sell meat and poultry obtain this produce from farms using methods in accord with food reformist principles.

Health food shops have always catered for the needs of food reformists, vegetarians, vegans, and believers in natural remedies. What these terms represent will be explained later (and see Glossary).

Every food store could be a health food store, making the term obsolete, if the fabricated deficiency foods that Dr Briggs condemned before the Senate Committee no longer dominated the diet of the people of the affluent nations. Ideally, all common foods should fully support health; but health-foodists believe that modern food production has strayed from that wholesome path.

The growing demand for health foods is recognised by many general food stores, which now stock some foods whose sale was pioneered by the health food shops, such as wheat germ, bran, molasses, yogurt, muesli, wholewheat flour products, and so on. Some large stores have special health food sections, and health food restaurants enjoy good support. Health foods are served in some students' restaurants. Health food shops, listed in the yellow pages in Britain and in America, remain the main specialist sellers of health foods, dietary supplements, natural remedies, and natural cosmetics.

Your daily diet

There are fashions in health foods as in so many things. Publicity is given to certain 'wonder foods', 'miracle herbs', or whatever – and there is a rush to buy. But what really counts is eating daily a balanced, nutritious diet. The basic principles of sound nutrition should be learned. They can be picked up from the chapters of this book and are summarised in the concluding chapter. All that need be said here is that you should base your diet on a variety of whole foods – for the nutrients work together as an efficient team – and any single food, herb, or dietary supplement, regardless of its reputation, should always be consumed in moderation. Over-enthusiasm could harm health instead of helping it. You can have too much of even a good thing.

Give health foods a trial, if you have not done so already. Include them in your daily diet for at least three months, and note how you feel. You should be feeling more alive, and enjoying your new diet as well.

Even a few changes in diet can improve health. Switching from white bread to wholewheat bread and from white sugar to more healthful sweeteners are two major steps in that direction. Taking brewer's yeast, wheat germ, or bran daily can often in itself bring improvement.

Cranks? There are a few. Exaggerations, of condemnation and of praise? Sometimes. But the health food movement is probably less guilty of eccentricities than many political and religious movements. There is genuine cause for public concern about the quality and the safety of mass-produced foodstuffs, and there are good reasons for people turning to a more natural and wholesome diet.

Dr Hugh Sinclair, who teaches nutrition at Oxford University, defines a health food as 'any food that retains all its nutritionally desirable constituents and has not had added any substance that is harmful'. What could be more reasonable or more health-minded than to base your diet on such foods?

Light on Sweetness

Molasses sugar – Molasses – Jaggery or 'Gur' –
Maple Syrup – Honey

Health foodists are opposed to the consumption of refined white sugar, and turn instead to raw molasses sugar, which is dark brown in colour, blackstrap molasses, honey, and natural maple syrup, and to the natural sugars abundant in fresh and dried fruits, vegetables, milk, and other foods.

What are sugars?

Sugar generally means sucrose, obtained mainly from sugar cane and sugar beet. But to the chemist the term covers a group of carbohydrates – which means that they are composed of three elements: carbon, hydrogen and oxygen, the ratio of the hydrogen and oxygen being the same as in water. All of the sugars are carbohydrates, and refined sugar is pure carbohydrate.

Chemically, there are two different kinds of sugars, which are classified as monosaccharides or disaccharides.

Monosaccharides, as their name indicates, are composed of one saccharide. Glucose is the sugar present in the blood and in some fruits and vegetables. Fructose, the sweetest of the sugars, is found in ripe fruits and in vegetables. Galactose is present in milk.

Maltose, lactose, and sucrose are disaccharides. Maltose is produced when saliva acts upon starch. Lactose is present in the milk of mammals. Sucrose is manufactured in green plants through the action of the energy in sunlight on the leaves, the process called photosynthesis. Sucrose rates second to fructose for sweetness but is well ahead of the other sugars. Its highest concentrations are in sugar cane and in sugar beet, the two major sources of the world's sugar.

The discovery of sugar stored in the root of the sugar beet plant was made in 1747 by a German chemist. It is grown in temperate zones, chiefly in Europe, the USA, and Canada, and supplies forty per cent of the world's sugar, and the root contains 15–20 per cent sucrose.

Sugar cane supplies sixty per cent of the world's consumption of sugar, and grows best in the tropics. The cut cane contains fourteen to seventeen per cent sucrose.

The sugar story

Sugar cane has been cultivated since well before the onset of the Christian era. Its cultivation was observed by officers in the army of Alexander the Great during the Indian campaign in 327 BC. Chinese and Indian herbalists had long before then been using sugar medicinally, and it was eaten by the Chinese, Indians, Egyptians, and Arabs for many centuries before it reached the tables of the European rich.

Sugar did not reach Britain until 1264, and the first British sugar refining started only in 1554. Queen Elizabeth I was a customer for the purest white sugar then available called 'Emperor's sugar'. (A contemporary German traveller suggested that her liking for sugar could explain her blackened teeth.)

European explorers were fascinated by the plant with the sweet juice which grew in hot countries. They took plants with them to see if they would grow in the new colonies of the West Indies and in North and South America, and started an industry that was to make use of negro slave labour.

What was shipped to Europe was not the white crystals that are a familiar sight in our supermarkets, but a dark sticky substance that retained much of the nutrients in the raw sugar cane. During the seventeenth and eighteenth centuries the common people in Europe and the American colonists who could not afford white sugar used raw brown sugar or black molasses instead.

The first sugar refining plant in America was set up in New York as early as 1689, but the white sugar product we are familiar with today was not produced until the middle of the nineteenth century. From then on its consumption grew rapidly as modern technology made mass production possible. Sugar was refined not only from sugar cane but also from beets, which could be grown in temperate climates. By 1940 more than seven million tons of refined sugar was consumed annually in USA – nearly one pound per person every three days. Americans now eat 104 lbs of sugar per person in a year. As this figure is an average, it means that some Americans consume as much as forty teaspoonfuls daily, supplying nearly one third of their total intake of calories. The British now consume five times as much sugar per person as they did one hundred years ago, and in two weeks they get through the same amount of sugar they consumed in a year two hundred years ago. The inevitable result is a deficiency of essential nutrients, for pure sugar calories are 'empty' in a nutritional sense.

The more sugar a person consumes the greater the risk of a deficiency of the B vitamins, which are needed to metabolise sugar and starch. They are present in sugar cane and sugar beet, but not in the refined sugar crystals, and those contained in other foods in the diet are usually needed to metabolise those foods.

Refined white sugar is pure carbohydrate – 'empty calories' – that contribute virtually nothing nutritionally to the diet. To metabolise sugars, the body needs B vitamins and some minerals in which refined sugar is lacking; it therefore 'filches' them from the body cells. People who eat a lot of sugar are often deficient in B vitamins and in some minerals.

John Yudkin, Professor of Nutrition and Dietetics at the University of London, says that the increased craving for sweetness is a harmful addiction. In countries where sugar consumption is high there is a correspondingly high rate of heart disease. African tribes such as the Masai and the Samburu eat a high percentage of animal fat but no refined sugar and yet have no coronary disease. The introduction of refined white sugar into a more natural diet invariably harms health. Some studies have found that hospital patients with heart disease habitually consume more sugar than patients with other diseases. When laboratory animals are fed high amounts of sugar they develop high blood cholesterol, high levels of triglycerides (natural fats) and of insulin, and their blood platelets become stickier. When some human volunteers were given large quantities of sugar and were then studied physiologically, some, but not all, of them developed similar reactions to that of the laboratory animals.

Professor Yudkin believes that eating a lot of sugar leads to heart disease because it upsets the hormone balance of the blood. Researchers have found a correlation between high sugar consumption and diabetes, dental decay, obesity, indigestion, gout, skin trouble, and perhaps cancer.

Molasses sugar

Some of the light brown sugars are little better than white sugar, being made of refined sugar and syrup. They have been virtually denuded of the vitamins and the minerals in the raw sugar cane or sugar beet.

The real soft, raw, cane sugar or natural molasses sugar sold in health food shops, of which the darker the better, contains no additives and such essential nutrients from the sugar cane or sugar beet as the minerals potassium, magnesium, calcium, and iron, and the B vitamins which are necessary to metabolise sugar.

Molasses sugar can be substituted for white sugar in all recipes. It is superior nutritionally to the white or light brown sugars. Even so, it should be used in moderation, and molasses or honey are preferable as sugar substitutes.

Molasses

Molasses, also known as black treacle, is the dark syrup left in the vats after sugar crystals have been centrifuged off from the crushed sugar cane or sugar beet during the processes of refining. The crystals are dried and graded either large or small; the large crystals are used to make granulated sugar and the small crystals are used to make caster sugar.

The sugar cane or beet, growing in the fields, contains vitamins and minerals. These are stripped away during the refining processes that produce white sugar – but they remain in the molasses. From a nutritional point of view, the darker the syrup the better. Blackstrap molasses are particularly rich in nutrients and are a well-known health food.

What makes molasses a health food? It is one of the richest sources of iron; only liver and brewer's yeast will give you more, weight for weight. It is also rich in calcium, chlorine, potassium, phosphorus, and copper. It also contains magnesium and sodium. It is rich in the B vitamins, necessary for the release of energy from sugars and starches. It is an exceptionally good source of Vitamins B1 and B6, which contribute to the making of our red blood cells and to the working of our nervous system.

Refined white sugar supplies none of the B vitamins that are in the sugar cane and sugar beet and only trace amounts of a few of the minerals. Molasses, weight for weight, has about half the calorie rating of sugar, because of its water content. A comparison of the vitamin and mineral contents of molasses and sugar will indicate why the former is a health food and the latter is not. The figures, published in *Prevention* magazine, relate to one hundred grams of each.

	Molasses	Sugar
Calories	220	400
B vitamins:		
Thiamine (B1)	245 micrograms	0
Riboflavin (B2)	240 micrograms	0
Pantothenic acid (B3)	260 micrograms	0
Niacin	4 milligrams	0
Biotin	16 micrograms	0
Pyridoxine (B6)	270 micrograms	0
Minerals:		
Calcium	258 milligrams	1 milligram
Chlorine	317 milligrams	trace
Copper	1·93 milligrams	·02 milligram
Iron	7·97 milligrams	·04 milligram
Magnesium	·04 milligram	0
Phosphorus	30 milligrams	trace
Potassium	1500 milligrams	·5 milligram
Sodium	90 milligrams	·3 milligram

Health foodists think it odd that the nutritionally rich molasses, a by-product of the sugar industry, should be used mainly as cattle feed – an example of the way we often feed our farm animals better than ourselves. But it is available in jars and tins from health food stores. It will keep for up to six months in a cool dry place if the lid is tightly sealed. Stir it into warm water or milk; trickle it on to breakfast cereal; spread it on wholewheat bread; and use it as a sugar substitute in making puddings, bread, cakes, biscuits, and so on.

Unfortunately, the taste of molasses, which combines sweetness and bitterness in a strange way, is not enjoyed by everyone. With persistence, one can acquire a taste for most health foods, but molasses often defeats this process. In that case, the nutrients in molasses should be obtained from an alternative source. The taste problem usually arises from taking molasses directly by the spoonful, which is not a good way to consume it, even if you enjoy the taste. It will stick obstinately to the teeth and eat into the enamel if the teeth are not brushed immediately. Molasses should always be mixed with other foods.

Molasses tart

6 tablespoons wholewheat flour
4 tablespoons butter or margarine

½ pint (300 ml) molasses
¼ pint (150 ml) hot water

Prepare and cook pie shell using shortcrust or flan pastry.

Method   Boil molasses and water together. Blend flour to smooth paste with a little of the water. Pour on the hot syrup and stir. Return to pan and cook until thick. Add the fat and pour into the pie shell.

Jaggery or 'Gur'

This is used as a sweetener in India. It is also used there to treat rheumatism and intestinal disorders. It is made either from the juice of the sugar cane or of the palm, and is sweeter than molasses. It can be obtained from some health food shops or stores specialising in oriental foods.

Maple syrup

Some people dislike the taste of molasses, but can there be anyone who fails to appreciate the fragrance and flavour of natural maple syrup? This was the sugar of the early American settlers, and today it is poured over breakfast hotcakes (pancakes), waffles, muffins, and oatmeal in North America from the homes of the southern states to those of Canada and Alaska.

The maple trees are tapped first in the spring and the sap is caught in buckets as it drips from the trees. The sap is mainly water and flavourless, and it takes about eighty-six gallons of sap to make one gallon of maple syrup. The nutritive value of the sap can vary widely from tree to tree and according to the time of tapping. Analyses carried out by Dr Albert L. Leaf of New York, showed the sap of one tree may have five times more potassium and four times more magnesium than that of another tree. He reported in *Science*, 28 February 1964, that one ounce (25 g) of maple syrup may contain the following minerals:

> calcium – 40 to 80 milligrams
> magnesium – 4 to 25 milligrams
> phosphorus – 3 to 6 milligrams
> potassium – 10 to 30 milligrams

As with molasses, the superiority to sugar in mineral content is marked.

(Beware of the widely-sold artificial maple syrup, which is just sugar and water, artificially flavoured and coloured. Buy the natural product at a health food store.)

Honey

Eating honey goes back to man's earliest history. Cave drawings depict men gathering honey from wild hives, and archaeologists have found pots at least ten thousand years old that seen to have been used for straining and storing honey. It was used medicinally by Greek and Roman physicians, and is mentioned in the Bible. Honey was man's main natural supply of sweetness, until he discovered ways to make sugar from plants.

The mysterious, almost mystical, life of the beehive has fascinated many people, including the famous writer Maurice Maeterlinck, who wrote *The Life of the Bee*. Honey is made by bees who have gathered nectar from flowers. As they move from flower to flower the bees carry pollen on their feet so fertilising the flowers. Enzymes in our gastro-intestinal tract convert compound sugars into simple sugars, but in the case of honey the work has already been done for us by the bees. The secretion of their salivary glands converts the flower nectar's sugar – mainly sucrose – into simple sugars (monosaccharides). The honey, predigested and processed, is stored by the bees in the honeycomb in hexagonal wax cells of remarkable mathematical exactitude. The honeycomb may itself be chewed, but most of the honey sold today is prepared in liquid form from honey taken from the comb.

Honey is easily assimilated by the human body and provides rapid energy. Honey is seventy-five to eighty per cent sugar and twenty to twenty-five per cent water – a powerful sugar and carbohydrate concentration. Its energy and calorie value is high – about the same as that of sugar. But, unlike sugar, honey contains useful vitamins, minerals and other health-serving constituents. It thus makes an excellent sugar substitute in the diet.

The nutritive quality of honey is influenced by the types of flower visited by the bees, the amount of pollen the bees consume, the time of year the nectar is collected, and the mineral content of the soil in which the bee-visited flowers have grown.

Honey contains the B vitamins that are stripped from the crushed sugar cane or beet in making refined sugar: B1 (thiamine), B2 (riboflavin), B3 (niacin), B6 (pyridoxine), pantothenic acid, nicotinic acid, folic acid, and biotin. There is some Vitamin C, depending on the amount of pollen in the honey. The B vitamins metabolise sugars and starches, are good blood builders, and support the functioning of the nervous system.

Honey also contains the minerals aluminium, calcium, chlorine, copper, iodine, iron, magnesium, manganese, phosphorus, potassium, silicon, and sodium. Although there are only traces of some of these minerals the human body only needs them in tiny amounts – nevertheless they are essential, their importance only being recognised in recent times. Scientists are still researching their effects.

Professor H. A. Schuette, of the Department of Chemistry, the

University of Wisconsin, says about the minerals in honey:

'Of these newer essentials, copper, iron and manganese, there seems to be a larger quantity in dark honey than in light. From a nutritional standpoint, iron is important because of its relation to the colouring matter of the blood, or haemoglobin. We build haemoglobin out of our food, and it has a certain power, carrying that all-important oxygen to our body tissues. Were it not for its iron content, haemoglobin would not have this property of holding oxygen.

Copper seems to unlock the therapeutic powers of iron, in restoring the haemoglobin content of the blood in patients afflicted with anaemia. In other words, copper promotes the action of iron.

We don't yet fully know the advantages of including manganese in the diet, but we do know enough about the subject to appreciate that it is a valuable adjunct to the diet. Some are of the opinion that it functions more or less interchangeably with copper, or as a supplement to it, aiding the formation of haemoglobin in the blood. Others, however, hold that iron is helped in this business of building haemoglobin by copper alone. Yet they find also evidence in other connections to support their opinion that manganese has a very specific function of its own in nutrition.'

In addition to these vitamins and minerals, honey contains some plant acids – ascetic, citric, formic, malic, and succinic; the digestion-aiding enzymes catalase, diastase, inulase and invertase; various natural sugars, and some resins and gums.

Honey's age-old reputation as an aid in healing wounds seems justified and it is known to contain natural antiseptic and antibiotic substances. Germs need water to survive and to multiply. Honey absorbs moisture and is a powerful germicide and a natural antiseptic and antibiotic. Dr W. G. Sackett, a bacteriologist at the Colorado Agriculture College, tried placing various disease germs in a pure honey medium. All of the disease bacteria died, either within a few hours or within a few days. He had included in the experiment micro-organisms producing broncho-pneumonia, dysentery, fever, peritonitis, pleuritis, and typhoid. His findings were duplicated in laboratories in Washington, Ottawa, and elsewhere.

In various parts of the world honey is used externally to assist the healing of wounds and it has often been used for this purpose through the centuries following battles.

Honey is also used in the treatment of anaemia and weak hearts. Dr G. N. W. Thomas reported in the *Lancet*, how two pounds of honey saved the life of a patient suffering from pneumonia. The condition of the patient's heart was critical, but consuming the honey restored his heart beat to normal. Dr Thomas wrote: 'Honey should be given for general physical repair and, above all, for heart failure.'

Greater use of honey as a replacement for sugar could reduce the high incidence of diabetes, some doctors believe. Dr F. G. Banting, who discovered insulin, stated: 'In the US, the incidence of diabetes has increased proportionately with the *per capita* consumption of cane sugar. In the heating and recrystalisation of the natural cane sugar, something is altered which leaves the refined product a dangerous foodstuff.'

The ancient Egyptians dressed wounds and burns with honey and used it in their medicines. Hippocrates, the father of modern medicine, wrote of honey: 'It causes heat, cleans sores and ulcers, softens hard ulcers of the lips, heals carbuncles and running sores.' Dioscorides gave it to patients with kidney disorders. Pliny, the Roman historian, recommended a mixture of honey and water as a cure for fever; of honey, vinegar, sea salt, and rainwater to treat sciatica, gout, and rheumatism; and of honey and unfermented grape juice for nervous disorders.

In the Old Testament we find the story of how Jonathan obtained strength from honey when fighting the Philistines. St Ambrose instructed his disciples to eat honey 'which cures wounds and conveys remedies to inward ulcers'. The Prophet Mohammed said: 'Honey is a remedy for every illness.'

For many centuries honey has been used to treat stomach ulcers and intestinal complaints, sciatica, gout, and rheumatism. Honey and lemon juice in hot water is recommended for coughs, colds, and 'flu, and honey and warm milk is said to relieve bronchitis. A teaspoonful taken at bedtime is said to calm the nervous system and to promote refreshing sleep.

The mildness of honey's action as a laxative, natural tranquiliser, and absorber of moisture makes it a suitable remedy for children suffering from constipation, nervous overactivity, sleeplessness, and bed-wetting. Some mothers give honey to their children because of its tonic properties.

In Norway honey is mixed with cod-liver oil to make a healing ointment.

Dr D. C. Jarvis, who wrote his best-selling *Folk Medicine* after practising among the mountain people of Vermont for over fifty years, recommends a mixture of honey and apple cider vinegar for a variety of illnesses. He recommends chewing the waxy honey-comb (or failing that taking liquid honey) for disorders of the respiratory tract, for a stuffy nose, for nasal sinusitis, and for hay fever. (The comb should be chewed for fifteen minutes or so and what is left in the mouth is then discarded, as with commercial chewing gum.)

Honey and the athlete

Many sportsmen and women find that taking two teaspoonfuls of honey about thirty minutes before a contest gives extra energy, and that taking honey after great exertion speeds up the dissipation of fatigue. Confirmation that this is no trick of the imagination came from studies carried out at Sports College in Canada. Lloyd Percival reported in the *American Bee Journal* (Hamilton, Ill.) October 1955 how various foods were tested for their ability to boost energy before athletic activity and to aid recovery afterwards. Other factors assessed included digestibility, chemical reaction (acidity, etc.), general tolerance, caloric content, taste appeal, and economy.

Honey proved the most successful of the foods tested, receiving a score of nine out of a possible ten points. There followed: glucose, $7\frac{1}{2}$; corn syrup, 7; brown sugar, 6; and white sugar, $4\frac{1}{2}$.

Mr Percival wrote:

'An analysis of our experience shows that: 1. Honey, so far as can be measured, supplies in an ideal way all the necessary energy requirements of the athlete for pre-activity fuelling up; for the sustaining of effort during activity; for quick energy recovery after effort. 2. Honey, with its high caloric content, can build up energy with smaller servings. 3. It is extremely popular (by far the most popular) with athletes, due to its taste appeal. 4. More honey can be tolerated by the average athlete than any other of the energy foods and beverages tested. 5. Versatility makes it popular, since it can be used in many ways, and in combination with other foods and beverages. 6. It is a pure food, apparently free from bacteria and irritating substances.

As a result we recommend honey: 1. To be used in pre-activity meals. 2. For use after activity. 3. As a rest-period "jack-up" during activity. 4. In the daily diet, especially for breakfast, in order to supply daily energy needs. 5. As a general sweetener and spread. 6. In combination with such foods as fruit salad, yogurt, custards, rice pudding, etc. 7. As a baking and food preparation sweetener. 8. In making candy. 9. Generally, instead of other types of sweeteners.' [*American Bee Journal*, October 1955]

The athletes tested were given two teaspoonfuls of honey thirty minutes before the test began. Performances fell when the honey was not taken.

The Canadian study led to the following general conclusions:

'Sports College has no hesitation in saying that, because of the general experience with honey over a period of four years, honey is an ideal energy and fatigue recovery fuel. We recommend it for all athletically active people, and for all those who are interested in sustaining a high energy level throughout the day.'

Uses

Honey can be used just as it is, spread on wholegrain bread or toast, pancakes, waffles, muffins, and so on. Creamed honey is available which can be used like butter, or you can make your own spread by adding butter or margarine and whipped cream to liquid honey: this is sometimes called Swiss honey.

Honey may also be used to sweeten breakfast cereals and desserts, in making bread, cakes, and tarts, and in cooking as a sugar substitute. It helps keep baked foods moist and prevents early staling. When baking with honey, use a quarter less than you would sugar and reduce by about a fifth the amount of liquid in any recipe. It can also be used in salad dressing and it blends well with yogurt if a sweetener is desired. It can be stirred into hot or cold drinks (shakes). Gayelord Hauser, in his book *Look Younger, Live Longer*, gives recipes for 'fortified fruit drinks' which include either a teaspoonful or a tablespoonful of honey. Among his suggestions for drinks that give quick additional energy is to shake or mix until smooth or frothy a glass of orange juice with two tablespoons of powdered skim milk and one tablespoon of honey. (Unsweetened pineapple juice may be used instead of orange juice.)

Do not keep honey in a refrigerator, and always keep the lid screwed on firmly. If the honey crystallises, place the jar in warm – not hot – water until the crystals disperse.

Flavours

Tiny amounts of volatile substances from the flowers' pollen give honey its many distinctive flavours. More than five hundred flowers supply nectar for bees, and, as the bees are likely to visit several flowers, the varieties of honey are many. According to season, one type of nectar may predominate giving honey its distinctive fragrance, flavour, colour, and texture: apple and hawthorn in the spring; white clover in the early summer; heather, the last of the year, but producing dark and delicious honey.

Much honey sold in supermarkets is a mixture of imported honeys that have been warmed and creamed to a bland uniformity. Go for the genuine individual honeys; exploring their flavours and subtle variations in colour and texture can be an adventure for the taste buds. In addition to those already mentioned, lavender, lime, orange blossom, wild rose, and many others are worth investigating.

Honey's benefits in summary

Honey's advantages over refined sugar should now be clear. Here is a summary:

1 Having been predigested by the bees, honey is easily and quickly assimilated by the body.
2 Honey supplies rapid energy – and also vitamins, minerals, and other nutrients.
3 Honey makes a good energiser for the athlete. It will provide energy before a contest and speed up recovery after exertion.
4 Honey does not irritate the lining of the digestive tract.
5 The kidneys find it easier to deal with honey than with sugar.
6 Honey calms an overactive nervous system.

7   Honey promotes relaxation and refreshing sleep.

8   Honey acts as a gentle natural laxative.

9   Honey is a germicide: applied externally, it will aid the healing of burns, bruises, and wounds.

10   Honey purifies the bloodstream and acts as a natural antibiotic.

11   Honey may be taken to prevent or relieve coughs and colds, sore throats, stuffy noses, hay fever, and respiratory disorders. Its reputation as a remedy for nervous disorders goes back hundreds of years.

12   Honey's flavour is stronger and more distinctive than that of sugar, and so one is less likely to overeat it.

13   Honey's flavours are derived from more than five hundred flowers visited by bees, so their range is great and a delightful exploration for the taste buds. In contrast, the taste of sugar is unvarying and unexciting.

14   Honey can be used as a substitute for sugar – trickled on cereals and desserts, in drinks, and in cooking.

Synthetic sweeteners

Powerful synthetic sweeteners, such as saccharin (ortho-sulpho-benzimide), were discovered in America in the late nineteenth century. They are five to six hundred times as sweet as sugar.

Cyclamate is another American discovery and is about thirty times as sweet as sugar. This was first used in America in 1950 and in Britain in 1964, but was banned in both countries in 1969 after it had been found that large doses could produce cancer of the bladder in rats.

Saccharin is also suspect and some governments have imposed limits on its use.

Perhaps more promising are the discoveries of powerful natural alternatives to sugar such as thaumatin and monellin, proteins isolated from the African thaumotococcus and dioscoreophyllum berries respectively. Thaumatin is four thousand times as sweet as sugar.

Sweetness in moderation

Cutting down on sugar crystals – even down and out – is to the advantage of health. When sweetness is required, use the sugar substitutes suggested in this chapter. But even these should be used in moderation.

Though in this chapter I have stressed the nutritional superiority of molasses sugar, molasses, natural maple syrup, and honey over refined sugar, resist the temptation to eat large quantities of any sweetener. They have their place in the total diet, but because their calorie content is high, and because the body converts other foods into sugar, care should be taken that their contribution to daily calorie intake is low. This is especially necessary if you have a tendency to put on weight easily.

Most people today do not expend energy to anything near the extent of earlier generations as more jobs today are automated and sedentary and, as a result, it is very easy to take in more fuel than is burned up in physical activity. The result is obesity and disorders and diseases associated with being overweight. It is important that calorie intake should match calorie expenditure through physical activity, thus keeping body weight stable.

It is also important that daily calorie intake should come from foods that give good nutritional value and are not just suppliers of 'empty' calories.

For most people in the West getting enough fuel from food is not a problem. They are more likely to have the problem of matching fuel supply with energy expenditure. There are carbohydrate foods other than sugar, which supply energy. Fats and proteins can be changed into sugar in the body to provide energy. Sixty-eight per cent of the food you eat becomes sugar in your body and is used to produce energy. The rest is used for building and repair.

Natural sugars are present in fruits, vegetables, milk and other foods. There is no better way of obtaining sugar than by eating grapes. Dried fruits are concentrated sources of natural sugars. These foods supply valuable nutrients as well as energy – their calories are not 'empty'.

Excessive intake of sugar from natural sources is almost impossible because of their strong distinctive flavours. (To make one comparison: you would need to eat six apples to obtain the amount of sugar the average tea-with-sugar drinker would take with a pot of tea.) But refined sugar and the many foods containing it have a mild bland sweet flavour that induces an automatic craving for more and causes over-consumption.

Millions of people are addicted to sugar, and it is an addiction that threatens their health. 'We have got so much into the habit of eating sweet foods that we go on eating them even when we have already got all the calories we need,' writes Professor John Yudkin in *This Slimming Business*.

'... I believe that the increase [in the consumption of] sugar is *not* the result of an instinct at all. I believe that it is just that we have developed a liking for it, an addiction, which makes us eat more and more even though we don't need it. I believe that at least some of the high amount of fat we eat comes about because of the use of sugar with fat in such foods as cakes, ice cream, and other sorts of confectionery. Sugar thus becomes a fat carrier, as well as providing calories itself.'

Remember that the over-consumption of refined concentrated carbohydrate foods, especially of sugar, is thought by many experts to be a major contributing factor to the high incidence in affluent countries of obesity, high blood pressure, heart disease, diabetes, diverticulitis, tooth decay, and other diseases and disorders.

You should cut down on the use of sugar crystals and on the many canned and processed foods which contain refined sugar. Read the labels. Food manufacturers make copious use of refined sugar.

Health food shops sell wholesome snack bars – confectionery made from healthful natural foods like honey, cereals, seeds, nuts, and so on. Carob, a sweet bean, makes an excellent substitute for chocolate.

Having 'a sweet tooth' should be cause for alarm and for a reappraisal of the nature of your diet. A craving for sweet foods is a call for curbing the consumption of sugar and for ensuring that sweetness comes only – and in moderation – from foods that are nutritionally valuable and not just suppliers of energy (calories).

Not only is health safeguarded by cutting right down on the intake of sugar – there is a bonus. Sugar's sweetness dominates whatever it is in, cloyingly masking the real flavour of the food or drink. So in cutting sugar consumption there is the opportunity to gain or regain knowledge of the true flavour of foods.

A few more cautionary words about the sweeteners. They will stick to your teeth and attack the enamel if you do not brush your teeth shortly after taking them. For this reason it is usually best to mix them with other foods and not take them directly by the spoonful. Even if you haven't a toothbrush to hand, it is usually possible to swish water around in your mouth. Your protective tooth enamel is itself worth protecting.

With the safeguards mentioned, healthful sweeteners such as molasses and honey can make a valuable contribution to your diet.

The Good Grains

Rice – Wheat – Bulgur – Buckwheat – Maize –
Barley – Millet – Sorghum – Oats – Rye

Observe any long grasses in late summer and you will see the seeds that form at the tops of the plants. Grains, often referred to as cereals (from Ceres, the Roman goddess of crops), are the seeds of domestic grasses, first cultivated many thousands of years ago. At some stage in human history it was discovered that if grains were moistened and kept in a warm place they quickly sprouted and if planted in the spring they kept on growing. The harvested grains could be kept during the winter for planting in the spring. This discovery was important, for it meant that previously nomadic groups were able to set up permanent settlements, instead of roaming in search of food.

Grains provide the bulk of man's food. No wonder that for many centuries harvest festivals have been celebrated throughout the world. Which grains a people eats normally depends on the prevailing climate. In temperate zones the main crops are wheat, barley, oats and rye. People in the tropics and sub-tropics eat rice, maize and millet. The type of grain determines whether it is eaten as loaves of bread, flat breads, porridges, gruels, and so on.

Grains provide as much as ninety per cent of the total calories of people in parts of Asia and Africa. In Western countries they provide about twenty-five per cent of daily calorie intake, consumed as breads, breakfast cereals, macaroni, spaghetti, and so on.

Grains have long been used throughout the world to make alcoholic drinks. Barley is used for brewing beer and for distilling whisky. Rye and bourbon whisky are made in the USA and Canada. Rice is used to make saké in Japan.

The approximate figures for world production of grains are as follows: rice 360 million tonnes, wheat 355 million tonnes, maize 325 million tonnes, barley 150 million tonnes, sorghum and millet 100 million tonnes, oats 48 million tonnes, and rye 35 million tonnes.

Genetic breeding has produced many types of grain. Cross-breeding can produce hardy cereals that are very resistant to disease. A hardy hybrid maize – a cross between rice and maize – has been very successful in the United States. By 1960, ninety-six per cent of the American maize crop was planted with hybrid seed. Most Canadian wheat today is the result of crossing the 'Red Fife' (traditionally used by Canadian farmers) with an early ripening Indian wheat so producing wheat that is harvested before the frosts of late summer.

Wheat and rye are the main grains for making bread, which is such an important food in most people's diet that I am devoting a separate chapter to it.

Whole grains

The threefold structure of whole grains should be noted, for in refining cereals two valuable parts of the grain are removed.

The protective outer coating or *bran* is composed chiefly of plant cellulose and provides fibre needed for healthy bowel function. It also provides some proteins, B vitamins, and minerals. The importance of dietary fibre is discussed in the chapter on bran.

The main part of the grain, making up eighty to ninety per cent, is the starchy *endosperm*, mainly carbohydrate, but also containing some proteins, and small amounts of vitamins and minerals.

The third part of the structure of the whole grain is the *germ*, and this contains the richest concentration of nutrients. It is found at the base of the berry, and is the part which sprouts when the seed is planted. It is rich in proteins, unsaturated fats, B vitamins, Vitamin E, and minerals, especially iron. Wheat germ makes a valuable dietary supplement.

In refining cereals, modern milling strips away the bran and the germ. This lengthens storage life, at the expense of a considerable amount of nutrients. Nutrients sacrificed include proteins, B complex vitamins, Vitamin E, and several minerals. The grains' fibre is also discarded. Returning some nutrients synthetically in the process, known as 'enriching', is inadequate compensation for the mutilation of the whole grain.

Rice

The staple food of more than half the world's population. Some authorities believe it was first cultivated in India, but the first record of its cultivation was in China in about 3000 BC. For more than four thousand years Chinese emperors and nobility took part in the annual ceremony of ploughing a rice field, and the Chinese equivalent of the English 'How do you do?' is 'Have you eaten your rice today?' In the East rice is a symbol of fertility and of happiness. In rural Japan there are shrines to the god Inari, the rice bearer, and the Japanese word for rice, *gohan*, means 'honourable food'.

The rice plant requires a wet, warm climate. It is usually grown in standing water, though it can be grown on dry land: it will grow on hills if the slopes are terraced.

World production of rice is about 360 million tonnes, and it is grown mainly in China, Korea, Japan, the Philippines, India, Burma and Thailand.

Rice dishes are also popular in Italy, Spain, and Latin America. Arabs introduced its cultivation to Spain and it has been grown in Italy since the fifteenth century. Cultivation of rice in South Carolina began in 1700.

Rice has a lower protein content than wheat and other principal cereals, but the protein is of good quality. It has a similar structure to wheat; and a similar devitalisation in milling occurs in refining it. The husk, bran and germ are removed and the remainder of the grain is polished.

Here Western technology and notions of refinement are not solely to blame, for Orientals themselves began the process of polishing to give rice an attractive sheen and to make it cook more easily.

Unfortunately, here again we find mankind robbing a fine natural food of much or most of its nutrient worth in the pursuit of dietary snobbery and mistaken notions of civilised refinement. The price that is paid for the pearling and polishing of rice is a considerable loss of protein, fats, vitamins and minerals. Unpolished rice contains ten per cent more protein, eighty-five per cent more essential fats, and seventy per cent more minerals than polished rice. And most of the grain's B vitamins are lost in the process too.

Experiments with a rice diet led to the coining of the word vitamin and the discovery of Vitamin B1. In 1897, Christian Eijkman was director of a laboratory based at a military hospital set up by a Dutch government commission to study the disease beri-beri in Batavia (now Djakarta). He noticed that paralysis in chickens resembled the symptoms of beri-beri. A microbe did not seem to be the cause. He found that he could precipitate this paralysis by feeding the chickens on polished rice and nothing else. He also found that he could cure the condition by feeding the chickens on the bran that had been removed in polishing the rice.

In 1910, Dr Casimir Funk of the Lister Institute of Preventive Medicine in London, fed pigeons a diet first of polished rice and then of natural, unpolished rice. The pigeons became ill on the polished rice and recovered on the natural rice. In the following year he isolated the factor from rice polishings which could cure beri-beri and coined the term 'vitamine'. In 1927, the British Medical Research Council gave the anti-beri-beri factor the name Vitamin B1, and in 1936 B1 was synthesised and named thiamine.

100 grams of cooked brown rice contains:

calories	119	Vitamin B6 (pyridoxine)	0·55 milligrams
protein	2·5 grams	folic acid	20·9 micrograms
carbohydrate	25·5 grams	Vitamin E	2·4 milligrams
fat	0·6 grams	calcium	12 milligrams
fibre	0·3 grams	iron	0·5 milligrams
Vitamin B1 (thiamine)	0·09 milligrams	phosphorus	73 milligrams
Vitamin B2 (riboflavin)	0·02 milligrams	potassium	70 milligrams
Vitamin B3 (Pantothenic acid)	1·4 milligrams	sodium	282 milligrams

The nutritional differences between types of rice available in stores should be made clear.

The most nutritious is *brown rice*, in which only the indigestible husk has been removed. Full value is obtained from the grain's protein, fats, fibre, vitamins, and range of minerals.

White rice has had its germ and bran removed as well as the husk. It keeps better than brown rice and cooks more quickly but the nutrient content is much reduced.

In *converted rice* the nutrient loss in milling is reduced. The rice is steeped in warm water and dried. Thiamine, other vitamins and minerals in the husk and bran pass into the endosperm, which is about three-quarters of the grain. The resulting grain is off-white rather than white.

Rice polish is the bran that has been removed during milling. As we saw earlier from experiments into the cause of beri-beri, the bran contains useful B vitamins.

Wild rice, which was grown by North American Indians for hundreds of years, is now cultivated commercially for its high nutritional content.

Rice flour includes some bran and provides a good contribution of B vitamins.

A few words about the *macrobiotic diet*. It is not, as far as my studies go, good Zen or Taoism, and certainly not good nutrition, to try to subsist on a diet exclusively of brown rice, or almost so. Rice contains no Vitamin A or Vitamin C. With fresh fruit and vegetables and brown rice you could possibly stay healthy, but why choose such dietary limitations? Zen teaching on diet is to make good use of foods well-tried over the centuries by people in your country – a very different matter from eating nothing but or almost nothing but brown rice.

There are numerous varieties of rice. Long-grain rice will separate when cooked and is best for plain boiled rice and savoury rice dishes. The stickier medium- and short-grain rices are better for puddings and stuffings.

Brown rice takes about twice as long to cook as white rice, but the health foodist should be compelled in choice by the former's undoubted superiority in nutrients, texture, and flavour.

Rice may be cooked in several ways. Boiling causes only a small loss of nutrients because those lost in the cooking water are re-absorbed into the rice.

Boiled brown rice

8 oz (250 g) of rice in 1 pint (600 ml) of water serves four people.

Add half a teaspoonful (2·5 ml) of sea salt to the water and bring to the boil. Add the rice, cover the pan, lower the heat, and simmer for about forty minutes.

All the liquid should be absorbed and the rice should be chewy but without a hard centre.

Vegetable stock may be used instead of water.

Many national rice dishes have become popular internationally and include Turkish *pilav* which has rice, meat, and vegetables, and is much the same dish as Russian *plov*, the Polish *pilaw*, and the Western European *pilaf*. *Pilau* is a Middle Eastern rice dish that is often served with kebabs. Spanish *paella* can contain a variety of ingredients, such as chicken pieces, prawns, mussels, bacon, garlic, and peas. *Kedgeree* is a rice and fish dish. India is famed for *rice curries* and Italy for *risotto*. The Scandinavians make rice porridge, and often sprinkle cinnamon over it.

In China and in Japan, and in some other places in the East rice is the main course in a meal and not an accompaniment to other foods. The traditional Japanese names for their three daily meals are morning rice, afternoon rice, and evening rice. In the East, cooking rice is a highly respected, even revered, art. Chinese cooks consider it important to retain the rice's natural flavour (*hsien*).

Rice may be boiled, fried, steamed or oven-cooked. The Chinese specialise in egg-fried rice.

Chinese egg-fried rice

8 oz (225 g) boiled brown rice
4 tablespoons (60 ml) olive or
cooking oil
1 medium-sized onion

2 eggs
1 tablespoon (15 ml) Tamari
or soy sauce

Heat the oil in a frying pan on a low heat. Add the thinly sliced onion. Raise to moderate heat and add the rice. Next pour on the beaten eggs. Keep forking so that the grains stay separate and are coated with egg. Tamari sauce may be mixed with the beaten eggs, or soy sauce stirred in immediately before serving.

Cooked brown rice is delicious served with melted butter and chopped herbs, spring onions, or grated cheese. In Iran, a dish of rice and chopped herbs is served traditionally at New Year and is believed to bring good luck in the year ahead.

Cooked rice may be served cold with salads and with other cold meals. Experiment with different flavours by adding chopped herbs, seeds, diced vegetables, and fruits. If desired, the rice may first be coated with a French dressing.

Combining soya beans or sesame seeds with brown rice provides a complete protein balance containing all the essential amino acids.

Wheat

Wheat was one of the first grains to be cultivated, and has been grown for at least ten thousand years. Earliest cultivation was in Asia Minor, the Middle East and Persia. It is a versatile plant that is grown today in many parts of the world. Plenty of water in the spring and hot, dry summers suit it best. Today there are winter wheats which grow in temperate zones. These are sown in the autumn or in early winter and harvested about ten months after sowing. Spring wheats are sown in the spring and harvested in late summer. Winter wheats produce more grain than spring wheats, but the latter is superior for making bread.

The first cultivated wheat that we know of was called *emmer*, and from this, through selective breeding, has come *Triticum aestivum*, used in making bread, and *Triticum durum*, used in making pasta.

It has been estimated that wheat is eaten in one form or another by about half the world's population. World production is about 355 million tonnes. The main growers are the USA, Canada, the USSR, France and China. It is also grown in Great Britain, Australia, India and Argentina.

Soil and climate influence the quality of the wheat. European wheat tends to be 'soft' or 'weak', which means that it is a little short in gluten, a protein which forms elastic threads when it absorbs water and which helps bread to rise. Europe imports 'strong' or 'hard' wheat from North America to use for making bread. The soft British wheat is better for making cakes and biscuits than for making bread. Wheats with different characteristics are often blended to produce a desired quality of flour.

Like rice in the East, wheat has long had poetic and religious associations. A field of ripe golden-headed wheat, is a beautiful sight – and it represents energy and body maintenance for millions of people. Being mainly carbohydrate, it supplies energy – the bulk of total calories for some people. And though its protein content is moderate, when eaten in sufficient quantities it supplies useful amounts of that body-building and body-repairing nutrient. Cereals provide nearly half the protein content of the world's diet.

Wheat contains more protein than rice, corn, barley, rye, or millet. Durum wheat has the second-highest protein content among cereals – about thirteen per cent. The highest protein content is in a newly developed cross between wheat and rye called *triticale*. This hybrid cereal has two per cent more protein than wheat, and also has a better balance of amino acids. It can be used in the same ways as wheat. Triticale flour makes nutritious bread, but the dough should receive only smooth, gentle kneading as its gluten is softer than that in wheat flour. Approximate composition of the wheat berry by percentage of weight is:

Carbohydrate	70	Fibre	1·5
Protein	13·5	Endosperm	83
Water	10	Bran	14
Fat	3	Germ	$2\frac{1}{2}$
Vitamins and minerals	2		

Refined wheat flour and its products, such as white bread, are made from the berry's *endosperm*, by far the largest part, about eighty-three per cent. It is mainly carbohydrate starch.

The *germ* is small in comparison to the endosperm and is situated at the base of the grain. It comprises only 2½ per cent of the berry, but has the richest concentration of nutrients. More than half the vitamins in the whole grain are in the germ, which is the part which sprouts. It is very rich in protein, the B vitamins, Vitamin E, and iron. This makes wheat germ a valuable dietary supplement. It is discussed further on p. 168.

Bran, which is fourteen per cent of the berry, is the protective outer coating of non-digestible fibre. Wheat bran, like wheat germ, is used as a dietary supplement, mainly for its fibre, which is lacking in the average Western diet. Bran also contains useful amounts of proteins and B vitamins.

The nutritional importance of making dietary use of the whole grain will be clear from the following composition figures, which show the amounts of proteins and B vitamins, as percentages of the whole berry, in the germ, the bran, and the endosperm.

Germ (*2½% of berry*)		*Bran* (*14% of berry*)		*Endosperm* (*83% of berry*)	
Vitamin B1	64%	Vitamin B6	73%	protein	70–75%
Vitamin B2	26%	pantothenic acid	50%	pantothenic acid	43%
Vitamin B6	21%	Vitamin B2	42%	Vitamin B2	32%
protein	8%	Vitamin B1	33%	Nicotinic acid (niacin)	12%
pantothenic acid	7%	protein	19%	Vitamin B6	6%
				Vitamin B1	3%

The whole wheat grain also contains choline, folic acid, inositol, Vitamin E, calcium, copper, iron, magnesium, manganese, potassium, phosphorus and other minerals.

Nutrients in 100 grams of wheat:

calories	334	Vitamin B2 (riboflavin)	0·17 milligrams
protein	12·2 grams		
fat	2·3 grams	nicotinic acid	5·0 milligrams
water	13·7 grams		
Vitamin B1 (thiamine)	0·04 milligrams	calcium	30 milligrams
		iron	3·5 milligrams

The Nutrient content of bread made from wheat flours is given on p. 75.

Wholewheat flour contains the whole grain including the wheat germ and the bran. It can be used to make bread, cakes, biscuits, pastry, pasta, and so on.

White flour is made from the starchy endosperm of the wheat. In milling the germ and the bran are discarded. (Farm animals benefit from these nutritionally valuable rejects.) Thirty-five per cent of the whole grain is sacrificed in the milling process, and bleaching with chlorine dioxide gives whiteness.

Under government legislation, flours other than whole grain (i.e. those of less than one hundred per cent extraction) are 'enriched' with some synthetic vitamins and minerals, though the final product does not have as much nutritional value as bread made from the whole grain, nor does it supply the removed fibre. In Britain, 'wheatmeal flour' is usually eighty-three or eighty-five per cent extraction and 'wholemeal flour' one hundred per cent extraction.

Wholewheat is cooked and processed to produce several ready-to-eat breakfast cereals. You can buy wholewheat grains and soak them overnight or grind them to make a cooked breakfast cereal that is good by itself or with nuts and fruit.

Wheat flakes may be eaten by themselves as a breakfast cereal or used as a *muesli* base, adding rolled oats, chopped nuts, and chopped dried fruits. They are the result of rolling, which facilitates speedier cooking.

Hard *durum wheat* is used for making the many varieties of *pasta*. *Semolina* is the endosperm of ground durum wheat.

Kibbled wheat The whole grains are cracked in a machine called a kibbler, so that they are broken into small pieces, rather than being milled. Kibbled wheat is used in making bread and breakfast cereals.

Cracked wheat The whole grains are cracked by pressure machinery. Cracked wheat cooks more easily than whole grains and retains most of the latter's nutritional content.

Sprouting Sprouting is a simple process, described more fully on p. 134. It can as much as double the wheat grains' content of protein, vitamins, minerals and enzymes. Wheat grains will sprout if they are washed and soaked overnight, then kept moist in a jar or tray in a warm place for a few days. Flush with lukewarm water three times a day. The tiny green shoots should be allowed to grow half an inch before being nipped off. Some people prefer tender shoots only the length of the grain.

The sprouts may be eaten just as they are, on wholewheat bread or butter or soft margarine, or with a salad. You can make a sandwich spread by chopping the sprouts and mixing them with a few nuts into a paste, to which may be added a little sea salt and freshly ground black pepper, a pinch of herb mixture, and the whole moistened with a little sunflower seed oil or other cold-pressed salad oil. The mixture can be rolled into balls and served with salad or on wholewheat bread toasted and buttered.

Wheat sprouts reach a satisfactory length in about three days, and yield four cups to one cup of grains. Other cereals may also be sprouted. The sprouts of barley, millet, oats, and rye are usually harvested at seed length, with a smaller yield than that of wheat sprouts.

Bulgur

Bulgur, which is partially cooked wholewheat, usually cracked or crushed, has a growing reputation as a health food, although it is not a new food. It's Biblical name was *arusah*: Ruth, the Bible tells us, served it to her family. It was enjoyed by Genghis Khan, and it has been popular in the Middle East, Asia Minor, and some parts of Eastern Europe since ancient times.

Its processing causes some loss of the B vitamins, but the lysine (one of the essential amino acids) is more available than in whole-wheat. Otherwise its content of protein, minerals, and vitamins is about the same as that of wholewheat.

It is cooked and used in similar ways to rice.

To cook: add one cup of bulgur to two cups of boiling water, cover and simmer for fifteen to twenty minutes.

It lends itself to a great variety of culinary uses. It will accompany meat, fish, and poultry dishes, and can be substituted for rice in such dishes as paella, pilaf and risotto. It can be used to thicken gravies, soups, and sauces, and in meat loaves, casseroles, and salads. It gives a special flavour to breads and pancakes.

Buckwheat

Buckwheat, also known as Saracen corn, is a grain-producing grass closely related to wheat. Its name is probably taken from beech wheat, its three-cornered seeds resemble beech nuts.

Though originating in Central Asia, it has long been popular in Holland, Brittany, and America, and is growing in popularity in Britain. The Americans make breakfast pancakes with it.

Buckwheat's heart-shaped leaves are rich in rutin, a bioflavonoid which is used by doctors to prevent bleeding caused by weakened blood vessels. For this reason, too, it is sometimes used in the treatment of haemorrhoids. Rutin tablets, made from buckwheat, are available from some food shops.

Buckwheat supplies protein, minerals, some of the B vitamins and ructic acid, which is good for healthy functioning of the arteries and the circulatory system. It has a high content of dietary fibre, 9·9 grams in one hundred grams of the whole grain. The same weight of whole-grain buckwheat provides 11·7 grams of protein and generous amounts of calcium, iron, magnesium, phosphorus, and potassium.

The husk of buckwheat is not so easy to remove as that of wheat and buckwheat flour tends to be more expensive. Dark buckwheat flour is rich in Vitamin B1 (thiamine), Vitamin B2 (riboflavin), and niacin, and supplies as much protein as the whole grains. Light buckwheat flour is a refined product with only half the protein of the dark flour and little B vitamins and fibre.

Buckwheat flour may be used to make delicious pancakes, biscuits, and muffins. The heavy dark flour can be lightened, if required, by mixing it with wheat or some other flour. Buckwheat flour is used to make the Japanese *soba* noodles.

Buckwheat seeds are hulled and crushed to make *groats*, which may be used to give texture to bread and biscuits or cooked and used like bulgur or rice.

Kasha is the name given to roasted buckwheat.

Maize (Corn)

Maize is the staple food of many people in Africa and in Central and South America. It was introduced to Europe by Christopher Columbus who took some to Spain in 1496 from Central America. The Aztecs, the Incas, and the Mayas worshipped sun-ripened maize.

It grows best in hot, humid, sub-tropical areas, but varieties have been bred that will grow in temperate zones. The USA is the world's leading exporter and about half the world production of about 325 million tonnes is grown in an area south and south-west of the Great Lakes known as the 'corn belt'.

Nutrient content per 100 grams:

calories	356	nicotinic	1·5 milligrams
protein	9·5 grams	acid	
fat	4·3 grams	calcium	1·2 milligrams
water	10·9 grams	iron	5·0 milligrams
Vitamin B1 (thiamine)	0·33 milligrams		
Vitamin B2 (riboflavin)	0·13 milligrams		

Maize's content of protein is less than that of the other principal grains except rice, and not of good quality (the protein in rice *is* of good quality). The nicotinic acid (niacin) in maize is in a bound form called niacytin which is not absorbed in the intestinal tract. A shortage of nicotinic acid causes pellagra, a disease which occurs in Africa, South Italy, South America, and other areas where maize is the staple food. The symptoms are unpleasant – dermatitis, diarrhoea, and dementia.

The Mexicans eat maize in the form of *tortillas*, which are flat cakes made of maize mixed with lime water. The soaking in an alkali releases the nicotinic acid from the niacytin so that it can be absorbed in the body, and the Mexicans have, as a result, been free from pellagra.

Nicotinic acid is easily obtained from other sources in a well-balanced diet. Foods rich in it include liver, poultry, beef, fish, wholewheat bread, potatoes, and mushrooms. Only a little is lost in cooking.

Maize is a versatile grain that can be fed to livestock, milled into flour, processed into cornflakes, eaten as a vegetable, made into cooking oil, turned into sugar, and used in manufacturing alcoholic drinks.

Maize lacks gluten, which means that dough made from its flour will not rise, but cornbreads are popular in Latin America and in parts of the USA.

Cornflour may be used to thicken soups or sauces or to lighten coarser flours. Coarse *cornmeal* makes the porridge which the Americans call *hominy grits* and the Italians know as *polenta*. Stone ground whole cornmeal is the richest in nutrients.

The enterprising Kellogg brothers made a huge commercial success out of processing corn into a crispy breakfast cereal. *Cornflakes* are rolled from maize from which the germ has been removed, though the manufacturers usually 'fortify' their product with synthetic B vitamins and iron.

Corn-on-the-cob is eaten as a vegetable: the maize seeds stay attached to the cob. Cook until tender and serve up buttered. The seeds stripped from the cob are also used as a vegetable and called *sweet corn*. The corn-cob is the shaft or central part on which the ears of maize grow; it is used to make the bowls of corn-cob tobacco pipes.

Corn oil is a useful cooking oil high in polyunsaturated fats.

Barley

The world's oldest cultivated grain? Probably, say some experts. It was eaten as a paste in Neolithic times, and it has been grown in Egypt for more than six thousand years. For thousands of years it has been used to make fermented drinks. It was so used by the ancient Egyptians, the Sumerians, the Babylonians and the Assyrians. The earliest known recipe for barley wine dates from about 2800 BC.

In Europe it was used to make bread until the sixteenth century, and was less expensive than wheat bread. It grows in similar areas and climates to wheat. Its importance declined as it was replaced by wheat, but it remains a staple food in some parts of the Near East, and is grown considerably in parts of Europe, the USA, India and Japan. World production is about 150 million tonnes.

Though a good source of protein, fat, carbohydrate, calcium, iron, Vitamin B1 and B2, and nicotinic acid, most of the world production goes either to feeding farm animals or for fermenting, beers, wines, and whisky.

There are two main types of barley in the West: *pot barley* and *pearl barley*. Pot barley has been husked but retains the bran and the germ. It is nutritionally superior to pearl barley, which lacks the bran, the germ and the husk.

Barley is used in baby foods and in invalid foods because it is easy to digest. Herbalists say that barley is good for the nervous system and recommend barley water, which is made from pearl barley, for kidney and bladder disorders. Barley wine, in small amounts, is also said to be good for the kidneys.

Nutrient content per 100 grams:

calories	350	Vitamin B2 (riboflavin)	0·20 milligrams
protein	10·5 grams	nicotinic acid	7·0 milligrams
fat	2·2 grams		
fibre	1·5 grams		
water	12·0 grams	calcium	35 milligrams
Vitamin B1 (thiamine)	0·50 milligrams	iron	4·0 milligrams

Barley can be boiled like rice and used in rice-type dishes. It can be cooked as a breakfast food and added to soups, stews and casseroles. Barley flour is fine and sweet-tasting and can be used for making bread and biscuits.

Sorghum

A hardy grain that grows best in hot, dry climates. It was first grown in Africa and in India, and is a staple food today in many parts of Africa and Asia. World production is 100 million tonnes. It is known as Egyptian wheat, *kafir corn* in South Africa, *milo* in East Africa, *feteritas* in the Sudan, and *shallu* in India.

Sorghum is of growing interest to health foodists because it is not usually refined and the whole grain is ground to make flour or meal which are rich in nutrients. It should be kept refrigerated to prevent rancidity.

Sorghum's composition is close to that of maize. The cane contains sugar molasses high in iron and laetrile (Vitamin B17), which some believe prevents and checks cancerous growths; but this is a matter of considerable controversy. (Millet is another good source of this substance.)

The grain can be cooked like rice and used in rice-type dishes or as a porridge. The flour can be used to make breads, cakes, and biscuits, or can be added to stews and casseroles.

Millet

'Millet is rightfully the king of all cereals,' says nutritionist Dr

Paavo Airola. Certainly this highly nutritious grain merits greater use in the West, other than for feed for poultry and cage-birds.

World production is about 100 million tonnes. It is a staple food in parts of Africa and India, where the whole grain is eaten as a porridge and as unleavened bread. It is used to make bread in China, where it was a staple food before the introduction of rice about 12,000 years ago. In India millet is known as *sorgo-grass*.

Compared with other grains, millet is high in protein and low in starch, contains more iron, digests easily, and does not cause flatulence. Millet and buckwheat are the only alkaline-forming grains; other grains are acid-forming. It contains lecithin, a trace element which helps keep the blood vessels open and healthy.

Nutrients in 100 grams:

calories	343	Vitamin B2 (riboflavin)	0·12 milligrams
protein	10·1 grams		
fat	3·3 grams	nicotinic acid	3·5 milligrams
fibre	1·5 grams		
water	11·1 grams	calcium	30 milligrams
Vitamin B1 (thiamine)	0·40 milligrams	iron	6·2 milligrams

Lacking gluten, millet makes only flat breads, like the Ethiopian *injera*. It can be cooked and served as a hot breakfast cereal; used in rice-type dishes; or can be mixed with other flours and added to soups, stews, and casseroles.

Oats

Dr Samuel Johnson, never slow to make a dig at the Scots, in his *Dictionary of the English Language* describes oats as 'a grain which in England is generally given to horses, but in Scotland supports the people'. His thrust will count for nothing with the health foodist, who appreciates the nutritional value of the coarser, fibre-rich foods and is aware that many foods given mainly to animals are of the highest nutritional value for both man and beast.

Oats are a hardy cereal that grow in temperate to cold climates and in poor soil. World production is about 48 million tonnes, with North America, Russia, and China the largest producers.

Some experts believe that oats originated as weeds in wheat fields, but this cereal is no poor relation of wheat or any other grain. Oats have a higher fat content than any other cereal and supply more energy – 385 calories per 100 grams. Further, the fat is easily digested. The British analysis of grain composition I have been using in this chapter rates oats top of the league for protein as well as fat, with 13 grams in 100 grams, though American samples tend to give wheat a slight edge over oats in protein. Oats are also unsurpassed among cereals in providing Vitamin B1, and its supply of Vitamin B2 is among the best. They are also a good source of inositol, iron, and phosphorus. They also contain the vitamins nicotinic acid and Vitamin E, and there are such minerals and trace elements as calcium, potassium, iodine, copper, manganese, and zinc.

Nutrients in 100 grams:

calories	385	Vitamin B2 (riboflavin)	0·14 milligrams
protein	13·0 grams		
fat	7·5 grams	nicotinic acid	1·3 milligrams
water	12·9 grams		
fibre	1·5 grams	calcium	60 milligrams
Vitamin B1 (thiamine)	0·50 milligrams	iron	3·8 milligrams

Oats are cultivated in Scotland and Ireland, providing oatmeal porridge and oatcakes. Oatmeal is made from the whole grain, rolled or cut into flakes. Processing results in only a minor loss of nutrients. Hulled or gritted oatmeal is nutritionally superior to steel cut oats.

'Instant' or 'quick cook' oatmeal has been heated before being rolled. Generally, the larger the flakes and the coarser the oatmeal the more nutrient content has been retained. Most of the packaged commercial porridge oats have been fined down for more convenient cooking; the 'real' coarse oatmeal takes long, slow cooking and patient stirring. Porridge should be served hot, with milk and molasses sugar or honey. Shakespeare wrote in *The Tempest*: 'He receives comfort like cold porridge.' Robert Burns wrote in *The Cotter's Saturday Night* of 'The halesome parritch, chief of Scotia's food.' The Scottish haggis, piped in ceremoniously at Burn's Night dinners, is made of oatmeal and offal. It comes as a surprise to learn that it was eaten by the Romans, though the Scots made it a national food. Other traditional Scottish oatmeal dishes are hodgils, an oatmeal dumpling, crowdie, which is oatmeal and buttermilk, an oatmeal sausage called a skirlie or mealie, and an oatmeal soup called brose in Scotland and brotchan in Ireland. Sydney Smith, in the early nineteenth century, called Scotland 'that land of Calvin, oatcakes, and sulphur'.

Oatcakes

8 oz (225 g) oatmeal
1½ oz (40 g) wholewheat flour
¼ teaspoon bicarbonate of soda
  (optional)

½ teaspoon salt
1 oz (25 g) vegetable
  margarine
hot water to bind
Warm all utensils

Put the dry ingredients in a bowl with the margarine in the centre. Add the hot water gradually and mix. Roll out on a floured board to ¼ inch thickness. Cut in triangles and bake in a hot oven for fifteen to twenty minutes, or on a greased griddle and finish off in the oven or under a not too hot grill to crisp them.

Oatcakes are delicious with butter and honey or with cheese.

The Scots make a cake of oatmeal and treacle called parkin. Oatmeal and raisin biscuits are popular in the USA.

Rolled oats make a perfect base for *muesli*. Other grains may also be used, and are discussed on p. 59.

Oatmeal tea

Boil two tablespoons of coarse oatmeal in a quart of water for an hour, then add the juice of two lemons and the grated rind of one lemon.

Rye

The hardiest of the cereals. Like oats, rye will grow in cold climates and on poor soil. Though it was probably first grown in Asia Minor, it has been an important crop in Central, Northern, and Eastern Europe since the Middle Ages. From Europe it was taken to America. It is a major crop today in Germany, Finland, Scandanavia and parts of Eastern Europe. World production is about 35 million tonnes.

Rye's protein content is one of the highest among cereals. Bread has been made from it in Europe since the Middle Ages, though it does not contain as much gluten as wheat.

Precautions are taken to make sure the ripe heads of rye are not attacked by a fungus called ergot which contains poisonous alkaloids, one of which is related to the hallucinogenic agents in LSD. Through the centuries there have been outbreaks of rye bread poisoning in Europe – the most recent as late as 1951 in the Rhône Valley, when several people suffered attacks of hallucinatory madness.

Rye bread is usually dark and dense in texture, and is highly nutritious. The German *pumpernickel* is particularly firm and black. Rye is also used to make biscuity crispbreads. Rye bread is popular in Germany, Scandinavia, Russia and East Europe. The British tend to prefer wheat bread.

Nutrients in rye per 100 grams:

calories	319	Vitamin B2 (riboflavin)	0·10 milligrams
protein	11·0 grams		
fat	1·9 grams	nicotinic acid	1·2 milligrams
water	13·8 grams		
Vitamin B1 (thiamine)	0·27 milligrams	calcium	50 milligrams
		iron	3·5 milligrams

Rye flour has a distinctive, slightly sour flavour. The health foodist will buy the dark flour rather than the 'light' flour from which much of the bran has been removed. In making bread, rye flour can be mixed with the flour of wheat and other cereals.

Whole grain rye is sold as *rye groats*, which can be soaked and then cooked like rice, and used in rice-type dishes. Cooking time can be shortened if the groats are cracked with a rolling pin or pestle.

Rye ferments quickly and it is used in some countries to make rye whisky.

Rye grains will sprout to seed length in three or four days if rinsed in lukewarm water thrice daily and kept in a warm place.

Muesli - the Health Food Breakfast

There is a health food way to enjoy the nutritional benefits of the grains discussed in the preceding chapter, plus the valuable nutrients in fruits, milk, and nuts. It is by bringing them together in the breakfast food known as *muesli* or Swiss breakfast.

The original *muesli* formula must be credited to Dr Max Bircher-Benner (1867-1939), who in 1897 founded the Bircher-Benner Clinic in Zurich. *Muesli* is now eaten as a breakfast cereal, but Dr Bircher-Benner gave it to his patients twice a day, in the morning and evening, and no other food at all.

He got the idea for his 'perfect food' from the raw fruit porridge eaten in fruit-growing areas of his native Switzerland. The porridge consisted of fruit, various cereals, and milk or cream. Nuts were sometimes added. The cereals used were mostly oats, wheat, and barley, and the fruits mostly apples, pears, and berries according to season.

It is so rich in nutrients that it makes a sustaining breakfast in itself. The cereals, fruits, nuts, and milk provide protein, fat, carbohydrate; the Vitamins A, B group, C, D, and E; the minerals calcium, iron, phosphorus, potassium, magnesium, and sodium; the trace elements iodine, copper, manganese, and zinc; fibre and other valuable contributions to the diet.

Muesli – the original Bircher-Benner recipe

To serve one person

1 tablespoon rolled oats or oatmeal

1 tablespoon (15 ml) lemon juice

1 tablespoon (15 ml) condensed milk

1 large or 2–3 small apples

1 tablespoon grated hazelnuts or almonds

The rolled oats or oatmeal should be soaked beforehand for twelve hours.

Mix the lemon juice and the condensed milk to a creamy texture. Stir in the oats or oatmeal. Wash the apple or apples, dry, remove stalks, grate into the mixture. Sprinkle nuts on top of the mixture and serve immediately.

This recipe should be looked upon as a principal melody on which numerous sets of variations are possible. Commercial packaged *muesli* is available, but it is less expensive and more fun to compose your own mixtures.

Ruth Bircher, in her book *Eating Your Way to Health*, advises: 'The dish should be light and fruity – a real fruit dish. The spoon should not be able to stand upright in it!' However, we are free to find the balance of ingredients and textures that suit each of us best.

'Instant' and 'quick cook' oatflakes need not be soaked – but bear in mind that they have lost some of their nutrients in processing.

Fresh fruit should be added just before eating. The original Bircher-Benner recipe recommended apples that are white-fleshed, juicy, and a little tart. Dried fruit may be chopped, minced, or put through an electric liquidiser.

All the cereals discussed in the preceding chapter may be used, singly or mixed, in orchestrating a *muesli*. And a great variety of fruits, fresh or dried, may be used. Experiment will reveal which fruits go well together. Ruth Bircher recommends the following combinations:

apples with
  chopped orange or
  tangerine, or bananas, or
  blackcurrants, or
  blackberries

plums, peaches or apricots,
  etc.
strawberries and raspberries
strawberries, raspberries and
  redcurrants
strawberries and apples

Sweeteners may be used. If you use sugar, make it dark brown molasses sugar. Honey is a better choice, and helps bind the mixture. Ruth Bircher suggests crushed linseed oil and honey (Linomel).

Nuts should be sprinkled on top of the mixture and not mixed with the *muesli*.

Condensed milk acts as a binder. So does cream, top of the milk, or yogurt.

The following groups of *muesli* ingredients could help stimulate your powers of composition:

buckwheat	apples	plums
bulgur	apricots	tangerines
corn	bananas	satsumas
millet	cherries	blackcurrants
oats	damsons	redcurrants
rice	grapes	bilberries
rye	grapefruits	blackberries
sorghum	greengages	boysenberries
wheat	guavas	loganberries
wheat bran	oranges	mulberries
wheat germ	peaches	raspberries
	pears	strawberries
	pineapples	

dried fruit:

apple rings	whole cow's milk	honey
apricots	top of the milk	molasses
currants	cream	molasses sugar
dates	skimmed milk	maple syrup
orange peel,	buttermilk	honey and linseed
grated	yogurt	oil (Linomel)

figs	plant milk	lemon juice
peach	nut cream	orange juice
prunes	almond purée	hot water
raisins		
sultanas		

The following recipe for *muesli* is recommended by the Department of Dietetics at the Bristol Royal Infirmary. At this English hospital Dr Burkitt and colleagues have carried out important research into the value of a diet high in fibre. No cooking is required.

1 cup of wheat bran	1 cup of mixed dried fruit
2 cups of rolled oats	½ cup of dried apple flakes
1 cup of chopped mixed nuts	

Mix all the ingredients together, then store in an airtight jar until needed.

Serve with fresh milk or yogurt.

You may add diced fresh fruit, such as apples, bananas, or peaches, to the mixture just before serving. Dried grated orange peel gives an interesting orangy tang.

Bran - the Friendly Fibre

In recent years bran has become a popular dietary supplement for thousands of people who would not otherwise class themselves as enthusiasts for health foods. This is in response to frequent references in newspapers and magazines, and on radio and television, to the way bran supplies the fibre lacking in the modern diet.

The media is reflecting a shift in medical opinion. Increasingly doctors are recommending taking bran as a way of preventing constipation and intestinal disorders. And some doctors are now recommending bran for patients suffering gut disorders; previously soft, bland foods, low in roughage, were prescribed.

Health foodists see this as confirmation of their long held views on the importance of roughage in the diet, which they obtain from whole grains, fruits, and vegetables, and a bran supplement.

Bran also contains vitamins, minerals, and other nutrients.

The importance of fibre

Fibre is not a positive health booster like vitamins and minerals. It is the non-digestible cellulose in plants. So why is its presence so essential in the diet?

Fibre adds bulk to the food passing through the intestinal tract, keeps it moving, and ensures regular daily emptying of waste material.

Diseases which may be linked with a deficiency of dietary fibre include: appendicitis, cancer of the bowel and rectum, diverticulitis, gall bladder disease, haemorrhoids ('piles'), hiatus hernia, irritable bowel syndrome, and polyps of the large bowel. Some researchers claim indirect links between a refined low-fibre diet and such diseases outside the gut as atherosclerosis (narrowing of the arteries), coronary heart disease, diabetes, obesity, thrombophlebitis, and varicose veins.

All these diseases and disorders are characteristic of twentieth century western civilisation. They are rare among those people (fast diminishing) who are outside contact with the modern refined diet and who have a well-balanced natural diet based on whole foods. Once they are introduced to refined low-fibre foods after an interval of some years, these people too, start contracting the 'diseases of civilisation'.

An appreciation of this problem was shown by Sir Arbuthnot Lane, an eminent British surgeon. In his book *The Prevention of Diseases Peculiar to Civilisation*, he wrote:

'The greatest of all physicians, Hippocrates, used to urge upon the citizens of Athens that it was essential that they should pass large bulky motions after every meal, and that to ensure this they had to eat abundantly of wholemeal bread, vegetables and fruits ... On this I can only comment that the modern doctor is not following the precepts and practice of his great predecessor, and that knowledge of diet has not formed an integral part of his education.'

There are signs that medical attention to diet and the importance of dietary fibre is increasing. Lawrence Galton, an American medical journalist, in his book *The Truth About Fibre In Your Diet*, writes:

'It now appears that with our modern technology we have once again outsmarted ourselves. By refining out of our diet an essential ingredient, dietary fibre – although it was not known to be essential before, and even the name is new – we developed the way for a remarkable variety of diseases, some of them chronic nagging nuisances even if not critical to life, others deadly, and all of them previously puzzling in many ways.'

Fibre highlighted

Credit for the fibre discovery should be given to three British doctors: Surgeon Captain T. L. Cleave, of the Royal Navy, pioneered the view that wholegrain cereals, vegetables, and fruits are essential for digestive and intestinal health and that the shortage of it in the refined Western diet is responsible for many current diseases and disorders. Dr Denis Burkitt, a member of the British Medical Research Council, met Dr Cleave and agreed with his ideas, which he propagated through lectures and articles in medical journals, and supported with research. Another who joined the campaign for more dietary fibre was Dr Neill Painter.

Peter Cleave trained in London and Bristol, and entered the naval service as a doctor. He served on ships, at naval hospitals, and, up to his retirement, as director of Medical Research at the Institute of Naval Medicine. His experiences on the battleship *King George V* during World War II influenced his views about dietary fibre.

Most of the 1500 men on the battleship were constipated, due to inadequate supplies of fresh fruits and vegetables.

'We had many tinned vegetables aboard,' Dr Cleave recounted, 'tinned turnips, tinned carrots, tinned everything. On one occasion I received a rebuke from the captain of the ship, a great friend of mine, when, at Scapa Flow, I saw sheep eating raw natural turnips, couldn't help thinking how much better off we would be on board if we had those turnips rather than the cooked analogs, and asked permission to land several thousand tins of our turnips for the sheep ashore while we took on board their raw manglewoozies for ourselves.'

He was constipated himself and decided to try taking unprocessed mill bran that was usually fed to animals. The personal experiment was successful and extended to all the men on board. He dispensed raw bran 'by the hundredweight'.

The daily inclusion of bran in the diet brought double relief for the sailors on board the *King George V* – relief from constipation and relief from 'piles'. Dr Cleave linked this disorder with the constipation: hardened faeces in the rectum pressed on veins in the rectal wall, producing the swollen blood vessels commonly called 'piles'. (It should be noted though that although the inclusion of bran in the diet brings relief, by lifting constipation, it cannot be expected to remove the haemorrhoidal masses.)

In 1946, at the Royal Naval Hospital in Chatham, Dr Cleave was working with a surgeon-commander who suffered from diverticular disease, in which small sacs (diverticula) or pouches form in the small or large intestine (colon), which may trap food particles and become inflamed and infected (diverticulitis). The walls of the colon may perforate and bleed, requiring surgery. It occurs most frequently in old age when the walls of the colon have weakened, and may be hereditary. Dr Cleave suggested to his colleague that he take bran. 'He achieved salvation with it.' Bran was then given beneficially to all patients coming into the Royal Naval Hospital who had diverticular disease.

Dr Cleave's views were supported later by Dr Denis Burkitt, who, as a government surgeon in Uganda, had discovered the disease now known as Burkitt's lymphoma. He observed that appendicitis, diverticular disease, and cancer of the bowel were rare among the people of rural Africa whose diet has a large content of fibre and high residue. Their food passes quickly through the intestines and their stools are large, moist, and well-formed. In contrast, the food of the average European or American is deficient in fibre, low in residue, and passes slowly through the intestines to produce small, dry, and poorly-formed stools. These observations Dr Burkitt and other doctors found significant.

Three doctors at the Bristol Royal Infirmary reported in *The Lancet*, 9 June 1973, how twenty patients were given thirty grams (just over one ounce) of bran daily without otherwise changing their diet, which was a typical British diet high in concentrated carbohydrates and low in fibre. Before the introduction of bran the patients' food was taking 3·8 days to appear as stools. After taking the bran daily, the time taken for food to pass through the body was reduced to 2·4 days.

In the following week's issue of *The Lancet*, Dr D. K. Payler reported the results of giving fourteen grams of bran daily to boys at an English boarding school. Larger stools and an increased transit time were recorded.

'This suggests,' Dr Payler wrote, 'that a return of approximately 2–3 grams of crude fibre [the amount in the fourteen grams of bran] to one's food each day may not only prevent constipation but might significantly alter bowel behaviour towards that which is characteristic of communities which are virtually free from non-infective bowel diseases and other ills characteristic of modern Western civilisation ... Here is evidence to suggest that this simple expedient might well do more to "keep the doctor away" than the proverbial apple.'

In the following week's issue of *The Lancet*, Dr Cleave pointed out that the stools of wild, vegetarian animals are odourless and those of the carnivores have only a mild odour. This is true also, he said, of people on a diet without refined carbohydrates. Sugar, in particular, he saw as the cause of offensive odour in stools. The odour could be reduced by taking bran and eliminating refined carbohydrates from the diet reduced it even more.

In *The Lancet*, 30 June 1973, Dr Neill Painter wrote: 'The evidence available supports Dr Payler's contention that a slight increase in our dietary fibre might lessen the incidence of certain large-bowel diseases. Surely, this simple experiment should be tried if we really believe that prevention is better than cure.' Dr Painter added that the slight increase in fibre could come from including inexpensive bran in the diet.

What is bran?

Bran is the fibre-rich protective outer coating of any grain, and is removed in the milling of white flour. Much of the bran is fed to animals, and some of it is processed into bran foods. The unprocessed bran is sold in health food and other stores, and bought partly for its nutrients but mainly for its supply of bowel-regulating fibre.

Dr Kenneth Heaton, in his preface to Jeanne Jones's *Fabulous Fibre Cookbook*, says:

'Fibre is the tough material from which are made the cell walls of all plants. All plant foods are rich in fibre, unless the food has been refined. Refining is any process which separates a fibre-rich fraction (which is generally thrown away or given to animals) from a starch-rich or sugar-rich fraction, which is sold as human food.'

Fibre makes us chew, but it cannot be digested by our digestive juices. It travels through the small intestine into the large intestine (colon) where its bulk acts as a gentle natural laxative.

Dr Cleave has pointed out that though fibre may seem inessential because it is not digested, its presence in the diet is as essential as that of the nitrogen, which also seems useless in itself, in the air we breathe. Air without nitrogen is pure oxygen, which is dangerous to the human body, as shown in the 1940s when many premature babies became blind when they were given too much oxygen in intensive care. Dr Cleave likes to quote Horace: 'You may drive out nature with a pitchfork, yet she will hurry back, to triumph in stealth over your foolish contempt.' Today, advanced technology, not a pitchfork, is used to drive out nature, and nature's revenge is more severe. Greater respect for nature and an understanding partnership is called for, not a jettisoning of the instruments of technology.

The composition of wheat bran will vary to some extent with the variety of wheat and the mineral content of the soil in which it grows. The following is one American analysis, free from additives:

Wheat bran – 100 grams

Calories	217
Protein	14.48 grams
Fat	3.15 grams
Carbohydrate	60·17 grams
Water	11·5 grams
Vitamins	
B1 (thiamine)	0·73 milligrams
B2 (riboflavin)	0·35 milligrams
B3 (niacin or nicotinic acid)	0·20 milligrams
B6 (pridoxine)	1·56 milligrams
Folic acid	0·13 milligrams
Pantothenic acid	2·45 milligrams

Minerals

Calcium	119·35 milligrams
Iron	15·05 milligrams
Magnesium	497·00 milligrams
Phosphorus	1137·00 milligrams
Potassium	1295·00 milligrams
Sodium	7·25 milligrams

There are 15–20 grams of fibre in 100 grams of bran.

Nutrients supplied most richly are proteins, carbohydrates, iron, phosphorus, potassium, and fibre. Also Vitamins B1, B2, B6, and pantothenic acid.

Uses

How much bran do you need? Whether one, two, or more table-spoonfuls a day is right for you is a matter for individual experi-mentation. How much you take will depend to a large extent on the amount of plant cellulose otherwise present in your diet. Fibre is obtained from whole grains, vegetables, and from fruits. Take enough to regulate your motions to your satisfaction. Hippocrates' aim of a bowel movement after every meal is unrealistic for most people, but daily consumption of bran should result in adequate bowel movements once or twice a day.

Unprocessed mill bran has a robust, nutty flavour that most people enjoy immediately or soon come to enjoy. It makes a good ingredient for a *muesli* or may be mixed with other breakfast grains and eaten with milk or yogurt and perhaps honey. Or you may wish simply to stir it into milk. Try sprinkling it on a dessert. It can also be used in cooking and in making bread, cakes, biscuits, and pastry. When bran is used in baking, either cut down on the flour or add more liquid. (See p. 76.)

For high-fibre recipes in general, see the concluding sections of Lawrence Galton's *The Truth About Fibre In Your Diet* or Jeanne Jones's *Fabulous Fibre Cookbook*.

Because fibre is chewy and absorbs water to become moist bulk in the body, it is likely that less food is otherwise eaten, a bonus for people who tend to put on weight easily.

Research has shown that the daily inclusion of small amounts of inexpensive bran in the diet will speed up the passage of food through the body and improve the elimination of waste. The health of the body is threatened when waste material stays too long in the bowels. But genuine health seekers will wish to make their diet one which includes plenty of high-residue foods. Some of these foods should be eaten raw each day. But the benefits from bran will be minimised if refined sugar, bread, and white flour products continue to be prominent in your diet.

Lawrence Galton writes:

'Bran, of course, contains fibre. But merely taking several spoonfuls of bran a day is not the answer because the evidence is that fibre in its natural state in foods has – as the result of being actually a part of those foods – effects and values not to be duplicated by bran alone.'

Bran is a superb supplement nevertheless, and one that few health foodists will be in a position to forego.

'Real' Bread

Wholegrain Bread – Wholewheat Bread:
its nutritional worth and how to make it

Health foodists are in no doubt about the kind of bread they want
– wholegrain bread which retains the bran and germ removed in
processing white flour. They prefer its nutty flavour and robust
texture, appreciate its nutrients, and fibre content, and the satisfaction eating it gives.

The firm, dark rye bread popular in Eastern Europe is filling
and nutritious. You can buy it in health food shops and some
other stores. But most people in the West think of true bread as
100 per cent wholewheat, for buying fresh and for making onself.

Losses in refining

Technological developments in milling in the nineteenth century
led to the denaturing and whitening of wheat flour on a massive
scale. In the eyes of many people, including nutritionists and

physicians, it was a disastrous change in eating habits for human health.

The composition of the wheat berry, and the importance of the bran and the germ, were described in the chapter on grains. We saw how the berry has a threefold structure: the outer coating of bran, the large endosperm, and small germ. The bran is unequalled as a source of dietary fibre, being composed mainly of plant cellulose. Lack of fibre or roughage in the diet has been linked by medical reserach with many diseases and disorders prevalent today in Western countries. The endosperm is mainly carbohydrate starch, but has some proteins and small amounts of vitamins and minerals. It makes up about eighty-three per cent of the berry. The germ is only $2\frac{1}{2}$ per cent of the berry, but is very rich in vitamins and iron.

The milling process produces flour. Wholegrain flour, which is what the health foodist is interested in, is the product of the first milling process. It contains the fibre-rich bran and the nutrient-rich germ. To produce white flour the milling process is extended and the final refined product is without the bran and the germ, with the nutritional and roughage losses that entails.

How great are the losses? Dr H. Schroder of Dartmouth Medical College made a study published in the *American Journal of Clinical Nutrition*, May 1971, vol. 24. The nutrient losses in refined white flour are given in percentages.

Vitamin B1 (thiamine)	77·1	calcium	60·0
		phosphorus	70·9
Vitamin B2 (riboflavin)	80·0	magnesium	84·7
		potassium	77·0
nicotinic acid (niacin)	80·8	sodium	78·3
		chromium	40·0
Vitamin B6 (pyridoxine)	71·8	manganese	85·8
		iron	75·6
pantothenic acid	50·0	cobalt	88·5
		copper	67·9
Vitamin E	86·3	zinc	77·7
		selenium	15·9
		molybdenum	48·0

Dr Wilfrid E. Shute, who has campaigned for greater use of Vitamin E for ailing and healthy hearts, is particularly perturbed by the loss of Vitamin E with white bread, consumed by most people in the West. In his *The Complete, Updated Vitamin E Book*, he writes:

'There have been many changes in our environment since 1912: the multiplication of food additives, the removal of essential vitamins and minerals from food, the pollution of air, water, and soil. But the greatest tragedy of all has been the removal of wheat germ from wheat, the stripping of flour and the "advances" that have been made in the manufacture of a basic staple food, bread. I am especially concerned with bread because this is the food which constitutes – or once constituted – our largest single source of natural Vitamin E.'

White flour is 'enriched' by the addition of synthetic Vitamins B1, B2, and nicotinic acid, and iron. Even so it remains inferior nutritionally to wholegrain flour. It is said that the lack of fibre can be made up by eating plenty of vegetables, but how many eaters of white bread do this? White flour and bread keep longer than wholewheat flour and bread, but this is only a minor problem for the consumer. Wholegrain breads should be either stored at room temperature or frozen; refrigeration leads to a quick loss of moisture and staleness.

Dr Roger J. Williams, an American biochemist, is a pioneer in vitamin research. He identified, isolated, and synthesised pantothenic acid, one of the B vitamins, and gave folic acid its name. In one of his experiments, described in his book *Nutrition Against Disease*, he placed rats on two bread diets. Sixty-four rats were given commercial 'enriched' bread, and a matching group was given the same bread but with a supplement of small amounts of vitamins, minerals, and the essential amino acid lysine. After ninety days, about two-thirds of the rats fed on the commercial enriched bread were dead of malnutrition and the others were severely stunted.

'The rats on the improved bread did surprisingly well,' Dr Williams says. 'Most of them were alive and growing at the

* From *The Complete, Updated Vitamin E Book* by Wilfrid E. Shute. Copyright © 1975 by Wilfrid E. Shute. Published by Keats Publishing Inc., New Canaan, CT. Used with permission.

end of the ninety-day experiment ... It is my contention that the milling and baking industry should have been doing experiments like this for decades, and should have been moving consistently in the direction of better bread by whatsoever routes seemed most appropriate to the experts ... Actually, "enriched flour" (it should, on the basis of the present knowledge, be called "deficient flour") is used in the preparation of a multitude of other products such as cakes, cookies, crackers, pastries, doughnuts, biscuits, muffins, waffles, pancakes, macaroni, noodles. All of these would be far better nutritionally if the flour were not needlessly so deficient ... I personally feel keen disappointment in the failure of the food industry to advance, because most of my scientific life has been devoted to exploring and increasing our knowledge about nutrition.'

The health of the American and European peoples could be improved if they consumed nutritionally better bread. More effective enrichment, such as Dr Williams suggests, would be a valuable step. But the food reformist hopes for greater public knowledge about the value of 100 per cent wholegrain bread. His objections to white bread are that:

1 The refined white flour from which white bread is made has been depleted of its nutrients. Twenty-six known nutrients are removed and only a maximum eight returned artificially. (The percentage extent of the depletion has been given above.)
2 White bread lacks the fibre that would have been present if the bran had not been removed. A shortage of fibre in the diet slows down the movement of food in the intestinal tract and the elimination of waste from the colon. A deficiency of dietary fibre has been linked with diverticulitis and other diseases.
3 White bread does not have the taste or texture of 'real' (wholegrain) bread.
4 Because it is not filling, white bread is easily over-consumed. As in the refining processes so much of the nutrient content is lost, this could mean that other more nutritionally-rich foods are crowded out of the diet. There is also the danger of causing overweight from the resulting high intake of calories.
5 For many years wheat flour was bleached with agene, chemically known as nitrogen trichloride, a component of gases which attacks the nervous system. Animals fed on the

bread containing this had fits and died. After decades of protest, its use was stopped. Food reformists are not happy about its replacement, chlorine dioxide. Chlorine was used in World War 1 as a poison gas, but the official view is that the small quantities used in bleaching flour are innocuous. The food reformist's objection to additives is the possible effects of their accumulated use over the years. Chlorine dioxide is thought by some to destroy Vitamin E, and some doctors believe that the chlorine combines with cholesterol to form deposits in the arteries.

Food reformists point to the fact that the accelerating growth of the 'diseases of civilisation' began in the 1870s, when steel roller-milling and the mass distribution of white bread began. They believe this is no coincidence. At the same time the consumption of white sugar was also shooting up, which may also have a bearing on the problem.

Stone mills were first used more than 2500 years ago. Heavy stones crushed and ground the grain. Roller-milling, invented in the 1870s, produced a radical change in bread-making and in the type of bread eaten by the majority of people. In this method the grain is rolled on cylinders and separated into three parts: white flour made from the starchy endosperm, the wheat germ, and the bran. The white flour is used to make bread and most of the bran and the nutrient-rich germ is used to feed cattle. In 1884 there were still 127,509 stone grist mills operating in America; by the end of the decade only a few remained in operation. The change to steel roller-milling meant the end of the nutritional loaf using the whole grain for millions of people and the mass-production of a devitalised white loaf.

The growth of interest in health foods has led to the reintroduction of stone grinding on a small scale in America and in Britain and Europe. The heat generated in stone grinding distributes the germ oil evenly through the flour, and even if the bran is sieved out, the germ oil will remain in the flour. In roller-milling the germ is removed by sieving.

More than one hundred years ago Sylvester Graham, an American vegetarian clergyman, campaigned for wholewheat bread and for natural foods. His campaign led to the formation in Britain of the Bread Reform League. Towards the end of the nineteenth century Dr T. R. Allinson added his voice to the campaign. He began milling his own flour and founded a company that continues to make wholewheat flour and wholewheat bread today.

In the 1930s the League of Nations recommended that more bran and germ should be retained in flour. An international conference was discussing taking action when World War II broke out.

Wartime food economies often lead to better bread and to better national health. During World War I the death rate in Denmark was the lowest in any European country after the government took the advice of Professor Mikkel Hindhede (1862–1945) of the Institute of Food Research and slaughtered seventy-five per cent of the country's pigs and switched the grain that would have fed them into wheat bread to which coarse bran was added. Within twelve months there was a dramatic improvement in the health of the Danish people and the two events would not seem to be unconnected.

The health of the British people improved during World War II, when sugar consumption was cut and the 'National loaf' was introduced made of eighty-five per cent extraction (white bread is about seventy per cent). (Due to a scarcity of wheat, Britain's bread did not become fully 'white' again until the 1950s.)

Wholewheat bread

Wholewheat bread is rich in fibre and supplies lots of energy and useful protein. It is a good source of the B vitamins which play a part in providing the body with energy by converting carbohydrate into glucose; they are also essential in the metabolism of fats and proteins. Because the B complex benefits the nervous system and digestion, Vitamin B is sometimes called 'the happiness vitamin'. A dificiency of the B vitamins leads to lassitude, irritability, neuraesthenia, and depression. It also supplies Vitamin E, and the minerals calcium, iron, phosphorus, potassium, magnesium, sodium, copper, selenium, and zinc.

One hundred grams of wholewheat bread – four to five slices – supplies 1·5 milligrams Vitamin E, 260 milligrams phosphorus, 315 milligrams potassium, 90 milligrams magnesium, ·30 milligrams copper, 77·5 milligrams selenium, and 2·5 milligrams zinc.

The appearance and elasticity of the skin is a good indication of health. Taking wholewheat bread regularly helps ensure an adequate supply of the B vitamins which are good for the skin. Doris Grant writes in *Your Daily Bread*:

'Every woman who wishes to possess a lovely skin – and who does not? – should remember that a sufficiency of Vitamin B in the diet prevents skin roughness and helps to create skin beauty. One of the best and easiest ways of ensuring a flawless complexion is to eat wholewheat bread. This bread not only supplies us with Vitamins B1 and B2 but with all the other B group vitamins in the right proportions.'

Nutrients in bread per 100 grams:

	White (enriched)	Wholewheat
calories	240	228
carbohydrate	51·7 grams	47·1 grams
protein	8·0 grams	8·2 grams
fat	1·4 grams	2·0 grams
water	38·4 grams	40·1 grams
Vitamin B1 (thiamine)	0·18 milligrams	0·20 milligrams
Vitamin B2 (riboflavin)	–	0·10 milligrams
nicotinic acid (niacin)	1·7 milligrams	3·5 milligrams
calcium	91·0 milligrams	26·0 milligrams
iron	1·82 milligrams	2·88 milligrams

Remember, though that some commercial brown breads are nothing or little more than white bread that has been tinged brown. Buy the 100 per cent wholegrain product, preferably made from stoneground flour, thus obtaining the minerals, vitamins, and fibre contained in the retained wheatgerm and bran.

And for real enjoyment, make your own bread, at least part of the time.

Making wholewheat bread

Is there a more warm, wholesome, and homely smell than that of freshly-baked bread? Its yeasty aroma fills the kitchen a few minutes after placing the dough in the oven and persists, though delicately changed, as the baked loaf cools on a wire tray.

To make your own bread use wholegrain flour, preferably stone-ground. Mixtures of wholegrains are possible, such as equal parts of wheat and rye flour, or half wheat and half barley. Three-quarters wheat and one-quarter oatmeal is another flour worth trying.

Rye bread is nearly always made from a mixture of rye flour and wheat flour. American rye bread is made usually from one-third rye flour mixed with two-thirds wheat flour. Wheat contains the highest amount of gluten, a substance which causes the flour to rise when activated yeast is introduced.

Pumpernickel is a firm dark bread made from unbolted rye flour mixed with wheat flour. A slice of pumpernickel (32 grams) can provide 79 calories, 2·9 grams protein, 4 grams fat, 17 grams carbohydrate, ·07 milligrams Vitamin B1, ·04 milligrams Vitamin B2, ·05 milligrams vitamin B6, 27 milligrams calcium, ·80 milligrams iron, 23 milligrams magnesium, 73 milligrams phosphorus, 145 milligrams potassium, and 182 milligrams sodium.

For extra nutritional punch, you can replace some of the flour with wheatgerm or bran. The latter will provide concentrated dietary fibre for healthy bowel movements. Bulgur or soy flour are also worth introducing. You can use honey or molasses rather than sugar, to activate the yeast. Using milk or buttermilk instead of water gives extra proteins, calcium, and Vitamin D. Some other healthful ingredients are egg, skimmed milk, raisins and other dried fruit, sesame seeds, sunflower seeds and so on.

The importance of dietary fibre has been stressed in this book. One way to make your bread high in fibre is by using some bran. The nutritious Bran-plus Loaf is made from wholewheat flour with added wheat bran. You will soon come to identify its texture and taste as that of 'real' bread.

The Bran-plus Loaf

To make two loaves

2 lb (1 kg) stoneground wholewheat flour

3 oz (75 g) unprocessed bran

28 fl oz (1 litre) tepid (blood heat) water

1 teaspoonful brown sugar, honey, or molasses (black treacle)

1 oz (25 g) yeast

1 level dessertspoon sea salt

Mix the salt with the flour and bran. Mix the yeast and the sugar/honey/molasses together and add half a cupful of water. Leave for ten minutes to froth up, then pour the yeast liquid into the flour and add the rest of the water. Mix well and knead for at least five minutes. The dough should feel firm and slippery, but not wet. Put the dough into two 'two pint' bread tins that have been warmed and greased with vegetable oil or unsalted butter.

Leave the tins in a warm place for $1\frac{1}{2}$ hours so that the dough can rise.

Place the tins in the top of an oven that has been heated to 400 °F. (Gas Mark 6–7). Bake for about forty minutes.

The baked loaf should be golden brown all over and sound hollow when tapped. It should cut easily; if the bread crumbles it is usually because the dough has been allowed to rise too high.

The bran holds moisture and the loaf will taste fresh for up to three days if wrapped in greaseproof paper, placed in a plastic bag, and kept refrigerated.

Some recipes include a tablespoonful of oil.

It is not just fancy to insist on loving care as important in the baking of bread, which has rich poetic and religious associations. Kahlil Gibran wrote in *The Prophet*: 'For if you bake bread with indifference, you make a bitter bread that feeds but half man's hunger.' Much the same could be said of one's awareness in eating bread.

Wholewheat bread and cheese makes a simple but nutritious meal, the limiting amino acids in the bread being 'completed' by those in the cheese. This combination also supplies fats, carbohydrates, B vitamins, calcium, iron, and other minerals. Wholewheat bread also may be enjoyed with soup, with salad, or with a chickpea or bean spread.

A final point. It is a mistake to think of wholegrain bread as a fattening food. Its bulk satisfies quickly and so it is eaten usually in moderate quantities.

Body Builders

*What are Proteins? – Amino Acids – Combining
Protein Foods – Meat – Poultry – Egg – Milk –
Yogurt – Kefir – Cheese*

Proteins are an essential part of all animal and plant cells, which means that the source of protein in the diet can be both animal and vegetable. In this chapter we will discuss the nature of proteins and what significance this has in planning a diet. This is followed by a discussion of the main sources of animal protein. Chapters 8 and 9 discuss nuts and pulses respectively, good sources of plant protein.

Animal protein comes from meat, poultry, fish, dairy products, particularly milk and cheese, and eggs. Plant protein comes mainly from grains, nuts, and pulses.

Proteins, which are complexes of simpler units called alpha amino acids, contain carbon, hydrogen, oxygen, and nitrogen, and sometimes iron, iodine, phosphorus, and sulphur. Not only is protein essential for human survival, it can justly claim to be the most important nutrient. Carbon, hydrogen, and oxygen can be obtained from carbohydrates, fats, and proteins; but only proteins contain nitrogen, sulphur, and phosphorus – substances essential for life.

What are proteins?

Proteins are the bricks of the human edifice, just as cellulose provides the supporting frame for plants. Our skin, muscles, tendons, cartilage, bones, nails and hair are made up chiefly of protein, which explains why protein is so important for children. If they go short of it, their growth will be retarded and their bodies stunted. Adults need protein for growth of tissues, such as hair and nails, and for repair of broken down cells. They will also provide energy when there is an excess of protein or carbohydrates and fats are in short supply.

Hormones and enzymes, which are vitally concerned with metabolism, are proteins, as is haemoglobin, which carries oxygen in the bloodstream. Another important function of protein is that it plays a part in the formation of antibodies which fight infection.

The amino acids

Planning a diet with a view to obtaining adequate usable protein centres on the patterns of amino acids. Amino acids are the simple units of which proteins are made. There are twenty amino acids. Eight of these are called 'essential' because the body cannot synthesise them, and so they must be found from the diet. The eight are: isoleucine, leucine, lysine, methionine, phenylalanine, threonine, trypyophan, and valine. A further amino acid, histidine, is essential for growth.

For protein synthesis, the body needs all eight essential amino acids simultaneously and in the right proportions. The patterns required are those close to the patterns of human tissues. Most protein foods supply all eight essential amino acids. Where then is the problem? The problem arises when one or more amino acids is present in amounts lower than the pattern requires. As a result protein synthesis may be impaired or even stopped altogether. Just as a stupid pupil can lower the learning performance of a whole class, so a shortage of one essential amino acid can bring down the performance of the whole eight to its level. This is literally true, for if an essential amino acid is deficient in amount by, say, fifty per cent, then only half the protein content of that food will be used by the body for its primary work of growth and repair.

Because of this phenomenon, there arose the widespread notion that a meatless diet is protein-deficient, as meat, poultry, fish and other animal protein foods have amino acid patterns closer to that of human body tissue than vegetable protein, which is often low in one or more of the essential amino acids. Animal protein foods are often described as having proteins of 'good quality' or 'first class' and vegetable proteins as being of 'poor quality' or 'second class'. These descriptions annoy vegetarians, for with understanding the problem is resolved. The shortage of an amino acid can be put right by including at the same meal another protein food which makes up the deficiency.

Cereals, wholewheat bread, beans, peas, lentils, and nuts supply protein, and any deficiency in one amino acid can usually be complemented by the inclusion in the same meal of milk, cheese, or eggs. Or the vegetable protein foods can themselves be mixed to balance amino acid weaknesses and strengths. The second course is that taken by vegans, who do not eat eggs, milk, cheese, or other dairy foods.

Any person going on a vegetarian diet for the first time should study nutrition, especially in the matter of obtaining adequate protein. This is particularly necessary if a strict vegan diet is envisaged. Join a vegetarian or vegan society and read their journal.

Protein deficiency, resulting in infected wounds and low healing capacity, was found in students at the University of California in the late 1960s and early 1970s, due to inadequate understanding of how to follow vegetarian and macrobiotic diets, in some cases compounded by fasting. Short fasts can be healthful, but understanding of the technique of fasting and of the body's nutritional needs are essential safeguards.

Usability the key

Frances Moore Lappé, in her best-selling book *Diet For A Small Planet*, says that, in considering the sources of protein supply, usability is a more important criterion than quality. 'Quality,' she says, is an unscientific term, and what is important is the amount of protein used by the body.

If we look at foods in terms of their percentage of protein content we have the following picture:

soybean flour	40·3	sardines	20·4
dried skimmed milk	35·2	egg	11·9
chicken, roast	29·6	peas, split	
peanuts	28·1	dried, boiled	8·3
cheese, cheddar	25·4	Bread, white	8·3
beef steak, grilled	25·2	milk	3·4
cod, fried	20·7		

There is a very different look to the table when the criterion becomes usability:

egg	94·0	tofu (soya curd)	65·0
milk	82·0	grains	50·0 to 70·0
fish	80·0	beans	50·0 to 60·0
cheese	70·0	nuts and seeds	45·0 to 55·0
meats and poultry	67·0		

Combining protein foods

You will see from the tables that egg comes nearest to full utilisation of its protein, and that milk makes a dramatic leap from 3·4 per cent content to 82 per cent usability. Eggs, milk, and cheese have superior protein usability value than meat, rice has the edge over meat and poultry, and soya curd (tofu) is almost as good.

Combining protein foods can increase the protein value of a meal. Including egg, milk, cheese, fish, meat, or poultry is likely to complement with their amino acid strengths the weaknesses of vegetable proteins. It can be a case of the whole being greater than the sum of its parts. Vegans should bring together a variety of vegetable proteins, so that a meagre amount of an essential amino acid in one can be supplemented by its presence in another food.

Fortunately, advantageous combinations nutritionally often please the palate as well. Bread and cheese is a good example. Bread's deficiencies in lysine and insoleucine are made good by their ample presence in the cheese. Macaroni and cheese, rice and beans, potato chips and fish, spaghetti and parmesan cheese, are other popular pairings that work out well for protein usability. Other useful pairings are rice and milk, peanuts and milk, beans and milk, potatoes and milk, cereal and milk, and rice and tofu (soybean curd).

Protein deficiency

Protein deficiency occurs when the staple diet lacks protein and what there is in the staple food is low in essential amino acids. For example, in places where the staple diet is cassava, which is less than one per cent protein, the results of protein deficiency can be seen. What are they? Stunted growth in children, muscle wasting, enlargement of the liver, lassitude and mental apathy.

When there is a shortage of protein wounds are slow to heal and are likely to become infected. Resistance to infection is poor.

Recommended daily allowances

Nutritionists vary in their recommendations for individual protein needs. Requirements are influenced by body weight, occupation, and other factors such as stress, illness, and pregnancy and lactation in women. The Department of Health and Social Security in Britain recommended the following daily protein allowance (1969):

Adult male   65 grams to 90 grams according to occupation
Adult female   51 grams to 63 grams according to occupation
Pregnancy   60 grams
Lactation   68 grams

Higher amounts of protein are required by people whose occupation requires considerable physical activity. The condition of the hair and nails starts deteriorating when there is a protein shortage.

Individuals can vary widely in nutrient needs. Each person can with benefit cultivate what Dr R. J. Williams, a nutritionist, calls 'body wisdom', which means becoming sensitive to how well you feel and how well you function. However, your awareness needs to be well-honed for several months to develop 'body wisdom' adequately.

Generally, American writers on food reform and health foods have tended to recommend more animal protein daily than their European counterparts, though it is rare to find any writers giving a clear decision on what percentage of the diet it should occupy. Lelord Kordel, for example, says that three meals a day should be based on animal protein. His own trial of taking 'only one medium portion of cheese, egg, meat, fish, or poultry a day' was followed by exhaustion. One wonders, then, how there can be so many healthy vegans, who eat no animal protein. It is not perhaps irrelevant to mention that meat is a mild stimulant and if used to eating sizeable amounts then breaking off or cutting right down could cause withdrawal symptoms, such as headaches, irritability, and fatigue; no longer taking coffee, tea, alcohol, or any other stimulant taken regularly has the same effect. These withdrawal symptoms are temporary.

It strikes me that the greater emphasis on animal protein – and this applies also to eating meat or not – between American and British and European writers on health foods might be explained by differences of national temperaments and traditions. The American, more extravert, go-getting, achievement-conscious ... and so on. There is not the space here to pursue this line of argument, and I would probably soon run into snags if I did. And the daily allowances for protein recommended by the American authorities are below those given above by British experts. Some readers may prefer the lower figures, so here is a table showing the Recommended Daily Dietary Allowance for Protein, as given by the National Academy of Sciences, of the USA (1974).

children (boys and girls) 1–3 years	23 grams
children (boys and girls) 4–6 years	30 grams
children (boys and girls) 7–10 years	36 grams
boys and girls 11–14 years	44 grams
girls 15–18 years	48 grams
boys 15–22 years	54 grams
males 23 years and over	56 grams
females 19 years and over	46 grams
pregnancy	+ 30 grams
lactation	+ 20 grams

Meat

Health food shops have always catered for the interests and needs of vegetarians, but food reformists are not necessarily vegetarians and many advocates of health foods eat meat, though often less frequently and in smaller amounts than average, due partly to the ethos of the health food movement but largely because they are prepared to make use of the variety of vegetable protein dishes. Most health foodists are aware of the nutritional worth of pulses, for example.

The few health food stores that do sell meat sell produce from animals reared in conditions free from those aspects of modern factory farming to which many people object on both health and ethical grounds.

Food reformist writers who are not vegetarians usually recommend moderate to low consumption of meat. Studies of long-life, good-health societies, such as the Hunzas, reveal diets based on natural whole foods with meat perhaps once a week or even less frequently, but with more frequent consumption of whole or sour milk, cheese and eggs.

In the affluent Western countries meat supplies about a quarter of protein intake. Meat's amino acids are well-supplied and well-balanced. All meats are good sources of the B group vitamins, especially Vitamin B1 (thiamine), nicotinic acid (niacin), and B12, a vitamin difficult to obtain other than from animal protein sources and which vegans often take as a dietary supplement. Muscle meat has only a trace of Vitamin A, but there are larger amounts in liver, heart and kidneys. Meats are good sources of iron, phosphorus, potassium, sodium, and magnesium, but are low in calcium. They have no fibre and little Vitamin C.

Offal includes such highly nutritious meats as liver, kidney, heart, brains, tongue, and sweetbreads, but they are high in cholesterol.

Liver is especially rich in nutrients. Cooked liver of all types furnishes rich amounts of protein, iron, and Vitamins A and the B group. A good helping of liver goes a long way to supplying the body's daily requirements of the B vitamins.

Pork takes longer to digest than other meats, but is rich in Vitamin B1 (thiamine).

Gelatine is obtained from the bones of cattle and is used commercially for setting jellies and sweets. Its nutritional contribution is low. It has only two of the eight essential amino acids.

The fat in meat in high in saturated fatty acids, which research has linked to narrowing of the arteries in some people. Women seem to be protected by their sex hormones until the menopause, after which their risk of heart disease becomes almost as high as men's.

Free-grazing animals tend to have less fat in their meat than those that are intensively reared.

Nutrients per 100 grams:

	Calories	Protein g	Fat g	Iron mg	B1 mg	B2 mg	Nicotinic Acid mg
Bacon, average	476	11·0	48·0	1·0	0·40	0·15	1·5
Beef, average	313	14·8	28·2	4·0	0·07	0·20	5·0
Beef, stewed steak	242	29·0	14·0	5·0	0·05	0·22	5·0
Lamb, roast	284	25·0	20·4	4·3	0·10	0·25	4·5
Pork, average	408	12·0	40·0	1·0	1·00	0·20	5·0
Kidney, braised	230	33·0	7·0	13·1	0·50	4·80	10·7
Liver, beef, sautéed with oil	230	26·0	10·0	9·0	0·30	4·10	16·5
Liver, calf	261	29·0	13·0	14·2	0·20	4·20	16·5

100 grams of calf's liver is a large slice. In addition to the nutrients listed above it contains 537 mg phosphorus, 453 mg potassium, 32,000 international units of Vitamin A, and 37 mg of Vitamin C.

The enzymes stay active in meat, which is hung usually for about ten days to give the enzymes time to make the meat more tender.

Meat should be eaten soon after purchase, and preferably on the same day. Frozen meat should be fully defrosted before use. Cook the meat so that full value is had from its nutrients. Much of the iron in meat gets into the juices during cooking and these should be used for gravies and sauces. Beef bones should be kept for use in soups, stews, and stocks.

Cook also to retain maximum flavour. People middle-aged and older complain that meat and poultry lack flavour. Forced fattening is partly to blame for this. In roasting meat you should preserve the flavour and the juice by using aluminium foil or a closed roasting dish.

The flavour of meat is influenced by its age and how it has been stored, the amount of fat, the type of animal and what the animal has fed on. The type of country on which an animal grazes can influence the flavour – highlands, lowlands, marsh, by the sea, and so on.

'Protein mythology'

Some vegetarians speak of meat as a 'dead' food, of an accumulation of possibly toxic juices, of the human alimentary tract not being the right length to cope with meat, and so on. But most vegetarians are so primarily for ethical, aesthetic, philosophical, spiritual, and ecological reasons.

The ecological argument is particularly powerful today, and has been cogently put by Frances Moore Lappé in her *Diet For A Small Planet* – a best-seller in America. Can we really afford to feed cattle on sixteen pounds of grain to produce one pound of meat, the other fifteen pounds becoming inaccessible to us? This is the kind of question many people are asking, at a time when millions of people in the underdeveloped countries suffer from protein starvation.

The alternative? Let Ms Lappé answer:

'By relying more on non-meat sources we can eat in a way that both maximises the earth's potential to meet our nutritional needs and, at the same time, minimises the disruption of the earth necessary to sustain us.'

Livestock are very poor protein converters. An acre of grain produces five times more protein than if the land is used for meat production; legumes (beans, peas, lentils) could produce ten times more protein; and leafy vegetables fifteen times more.

Frances Moore Lappé writes of what she calls 'protein mythology', which includes such erroneous ideas as that meat contains more protein than any other food (it comes in the middle of the league table as shown above); that only by eating meat can one get enough protein (daily requirements are easily met from non-meat foods); that eating meat is the only way to get 'first class' protein (we have already discussed how good protein can be obtained without meat); and so on.

Unscientific and exaggerated attacks on meat and meat-eating are sometimes made – just as, in the opposite direction, they are made on vegetarianism – but the ecological argument summarised above has a logic and directness that is difficult to ignore or to dismiss.

Meat substitutes

For people who are prepared to give up meat at least occasionally but who still want the flavour of meat, there are meat substitutes. Most of them are made of soybean, which is an excellent source of vegetable protein. Substitutes can be made to taste very similar to different meats, and go well with rice or potatoes. Some people mix the substitutes with pieces of real meat: combining in this way can act as a lead-in to use of the substitutes by themselves.

Poultry

A more economical and more easily digested supplier of well-balanced protein than meat, but mostly today the product of methods of factory farming that many people find repellent. Supporters of intensive poultry farming point out that it has led to a consumption of chicken meat several times what it was fifty years ago.

Tender chicken is the most easily digested meat. Chicken and turkey have more protein than fat, but the reverse is true of ducks and geese, whose fat content is mostly double their protein content. Ducks and geese also have a high content of cholesterol.

Turkeys, ducks, and geese are less subjected to intensive factory-farming than chickens, and their flavour is more distinctive than that of oven-ready chickens. Goose meat is popular in Scandinavia, Germany and Holland, but much less so in Britain and in the USA.

Chicken and turkey supply 220 calories per 100 grams and are made up of 63 per cent water, 20 per cent protein, 16 per cent fat, 1 per cent vitamins and minerals. There is no carbohydrate or fibre, but they are very good sources of protein, B vitamins, and iron.

Nutrients in roast chicken, per 100 grams:

calories	184	Vitamin B2	·15 milligrams
protein	29·6 grams	(riboflavin)	
fat	7·3 grams	nicotinic acid	4·9 milligrams
Vitamin B1	·04 milligrams	(B3)	
(thiamine)		calcium	15 milligrams
		iron	2·6 milligrams

Duck and goose supply 340 calories per 100 grams and are made up of 53 per cent water, 30 per cent fat, 16 per cent protein, 1 per cent vitamins and minerals. There is no carbohydrate or fibre.

Some health food shops supply free-range poultry which is superior in flavour to the mass-produced oven-ready chickens. The latter may be sprayed or injected with monosodium glutumate to make them appear less insipid, and during its short life of three or four months a factory-farmed chicken is often dosed with chemicals.

The skilful cook will preserve flavour as much as possible. Marinading, using herbs and spices, is a useful method of giving flavour.

Make sure that frozen chickens have thoroughly thawed before cooking. The cooking, too, should be thorough. Food poisoning can result from carelessness in these matters.

Brillat-Savarin wrote: 'Chicken is to the cook what canvas is to the painter.' Even so, French chicken farmers are not allowed to produce so many tasteless birds as their British and other counterparts. French shoppers can buy fresh chickens that began life in batteries but spend the latter part of their lives in some freedom and on a diet of maize. Such chickens are tied with red ribbons and described as 'finished with maize', '75 per cent cereal fed', and so on. Since 1957 the chickens of Bresse have been given an *appellation contrôlée*, just like a bottle of wine. They run about and scratch the earth outdoors, in at least ten square metres each, and are fed on maize and dairy products. As a result, these birds taste in a way which has become only a memory for many people middle-aged and older in Britain.

Fish

An excellent source of protein, vitamins, and minerals discussed on p. 156.

Egg

Egg contains all eight essential amino acids and is described by nutritionists as a near perfect source of complete protein, six to seven grams in one large hen's egg. It also supplies Vitamins A,

B1, B2, B6, B12, biotin, folic acid, nicotinic acid (niacin), pantothenic acid, choline D, and E, plus the minerals calcium, iron, phosphorus, potassium, sodium, manganese, magnesium, copper, selenium, and zinc. It is unrivalled as a source of choline, one of the B group vitamins and a basic constituent of lecithin. Choline has important roles in the healthy functioning of the liver.

Nutrients in raw fresh egg per 100 grams:

calories	158	nicotinic acid (niacin)	·1 milligrams
protein	11·9 grams		
fat	12·3 grams	Vitamin B12	·8 milligrams
Vitamin A	1180 i.u.	calcium	56 milligrams
Vitamin B1 (thiamine)	·10 milligrams	iron	2·5 milligrams
Vitamin B2	·35 milligrams		

All the fat in egg is in the yolk, which is also high in cholesterol. As cholesterol has been linked with the build up of fat on the walls of the arteries in some people, some medical associations advise eating not more than one egg a day and not every day. However, Dr Roger Williams, internationally known as a nutritionist, says in his book *Nutrition Against Disease*:

'Animal studies support the position that eggs consumed in large quantities in the diet, other things remaining equal, are not atherogenic. While both the cholesterol and lecithin of egg yolks may increase serum cholesterol levels – the actual amount *circulating* in the blood – the cholesterol/phosphorus-lipid *ratio* remains normal, and arterial fatty deposits are prevented from forming.'

The cholesterol content of eggs can be greatly reduced if the hens are fed unsaturated fatty acids, such as sunflower oil. Some people with heart disease eat only the white of the egg. Dried egg white is sold as a protein supplement: a tablespoonful stirred into a drink will supply about fifteen per cent of daily protein need.

Half the folic acid in raw eggs is lost in cooking. On the other hand, raw eggs contain in their whites the protein avidin which makes biotin unusable; but no problem arises if the egg is cooked, as heat inactivates the avidin.

Ducks' egg has more fat than hens' egg, just as ducks' meat has more fat than hens' meat. A hen's egg has about equal parts – 12 per cent – of protein and fat.

Health food shops sell 'free range eggs', which means that the eggs have been laid by hens acquainted with fresh air and sunlight and able to obtain mineral salts from the soil. In Britain today only six to seven per cent of hens have an outdoor run; the rest are packed into the small wire cages of the battery system or are on deep litter.

Analysis is said to show no difference in the nutritional contents of eggs laid by battery hens and those with an outdoor run. Whether this is so or not, there *is* a difference in flavour, the eggs of the latter having a more distinctive taste. (As a boy, I used to visit relatives who had a farm where the hens scratched and pecked at the edge of a salt-sea lough, and I clearly recall the distinct sea flavour of each spoonful of egg.)

Analysis also fails to show any differences between the composition of brown-shelled eggs and white-shelled eggs, though the idea persists in some minds that the former is nutritionally superior. Whether an egg is white-shelled or brown-shelled depends on the breed of the hen. Brown is superior to white when it comes to bread, rice, and sugar – but that is due to the stripping of nutrients in the refining processes. Hens, as far as we know, do not go in for refining on their own account.

Only a minority of people in industrial nations taste a really fresh egg today. The yolk of a fresh egg stays firm when the egg is broken, and the white has a milky texture. The shells of fresh eggs have a matt surface (as the eggs become older the shells become shiny).

Store eggs in a refrigerator, keeping the pointed end downwards so that the air space in the broad end of the egg stays at the top. If an eggshell is soiled, wipe it with a dry cloth; washing removes the protective film on the shell which keeps out bacteria and prevents the egg becoming tainted.

Milk

Mother's milk is the natural food of the infant, but soon he or she is drinking other milk. Since ancient times mankind has consumed milk from the cow, the goat, the ass, the mare, the camel, the buffalo, and the ewe. The milk has been drunk, fermented, and made into cheese.

Like the egg, milk is a near perfect food. It contains all essential amino acids in good balance and is a superb body-builder. It strengthens bones and protects teeth against decay. It is especially valuable for growing children. In addition to protein, it contains fat, carbohydrate, vitamins A, B, C, D and E, and is rich in calcium, phosphorus, and potassium. It is low in iron.

Nutrients in fluid whole cow's milk per 100 grams:

calories	65	Vitamin B2 (riboflavin)	·15 milligrams
protein	3·3 grams		
fat	3·8 grams	nicotinic acid (niacin)	·1 milligrams
carbohydrate	4·8 grams		
Vitamin A	150 i.u.	Vitamin C	1 milligram
Vitamin B1 (thiamine)	·04 milligrams	calcium	120 milli-grams
		iron	·1 milligrams

Though milk contains only 3·4 per cent protein based on weight, the percentage leaps dramatically to eighty-two per cent on usability, slightly higher than fish and well above meat.

Because milk is so well supplied with essential amino acids, it can complete the limited amino acids of nuts, beans, cereals, vegetables, and other foods, if taken at the same meal.

Milk's vitamin content varies between summer and winter. The content of Vitamin D in summer may be more than double that of winter and that of Vitamin A may have increased by more than fifty per cent.

Milk should be looked upon as a food rather than as a drink, and so be sipped and not gulped down to gather as a lumpy mass in the stomach. Some adults have difficulty absorbing it, and, as it may be mucus forming, it may not be suitable for people suffering from catarrh or bronchitis.

Boiling milk causes a loss of up to twenty per cent of its content of Vitamin C and storage causes a rapid loss of this vitamin, as much as two-thirds in twenty-four hours. You should also guard against leaving bottled milk in bright sunlight, otherwise about ten per cent of its Vitamin B content will be lost in an hour.

Homogenised milk has had the cream evenly distributed so that it does not rise to the top. Pasteurisation was named after

Pasteur, the nineteenth-century French chemist.

Pasteurised milk has been heated to destroy bacteria that make milk sour quickly. Some Vitamin B1 and Vitamin C is lost in the process.

Sterilised milk has a greater loss of vitamins: half the Vitamin B1 and C contents. There is another considerable loss of vitamins in ultra high temperature

(*UHT*) treatment to produce 'long life' milk.

Condensed milk is milk that has been evaporated and sweetened with sugar.

Dried skimmed milk is excellent value for money. The cream at the top of the whole milk has been removed, leaving milk that is low in fat, a half to one per cent. The skimmed milk is high in protein and calcium. It may be used to make low-fat cheese and yogurt. Skimmed milk powder is ideal for people on a low-fat diet, and, because of its concentration of good protein, higher than that of whole milk, it can be used as a dietary supplement.

Various nutritious *plant milks* are available, most of them made from soybean. Note that artificial milk products made from coconut are high in saturated fats, the coconut being something of a freak among nuts as regards its fats. Soya milk powder can be made into milk or cream simply by adding water. You can make your own plant milk by sieving or using an electric liquidizer, from beans, nuts, almonds, and pine kernels.

Though milk is one of the most complete foods, some adults lack certain lactases or digestive enzymes needed to split milk sugar (lactose). This occurs most frequently in black and Oriental people. Such an enzyme shortage causes digestive discomfort, but there is no problem with fermented milk, such as buttermilk or yogurt.

Yogurt

Fermented milk is a popular food in many parts of the world; it is called *yoghourt* in Bulgaria and Turkey, *kefir* or *keban* in Southern Russia and parts of the Near East, *koumiss* in Siberia, *tarho* in parts of the Balkans, *skyr* in Iceland, *pumpermilch* in Germany, *kunney* in Mongolia, *ojran* in Greece, *kumys* in Romania, *glumse* in Finland, *leben* or *laban* in Egypt, and so on.

The English-speaking West has adopted the name yogurt which

is now widely available through general stores and is not just a speciality of health food retailers, though it is looked upon as a health food.

Its popularity in the West is of recent origin, but for many centuries it has been part of the everyday diet of people in Eastern Europe, the Near and Middle East, and North Africa. As milk does not stay fresh for more than a few hours in warm climates, people long ago experimented to find ways to make sour milk palatable, other than by making cheese. Various vegetable and animal substances were used to trigger the process of fermentation. The acidity and consistency of cultured milk varied from country to country and from tribe to tribe according to which animal's milk was used, the method of fermentation, and the duration of fermentation.

The method most commonly used to make yogurt today is to introduce a live culture into sweet milk, then sustain the right temperature for the culture's micro-organisms to proliferate and convert liquid milk to a custardy fermented food. The consistency can vary from water to firm enough to stand a spoon upright in.

Yogurt's reputation as a health food is based largely on a belief that its consumption creates a healthy 'environment' for helpful bacteria in the intestines, one perhaps favourable to long life. Much of this reputation was due to the work of Dr Ilya Metchnikov (1845–1916), a Russian biochemist who won the Nobel Prize for Medicine in 1908. The year before, at the Pasteur Institute in Paris, he began to study yogurt, having been impressed by the health and longevity of people in the mountainous areas of Bulgaria and Georgia who were daily consumers of cultured milk.

Metchnikov isolated what he called the 'long life bacillus'. The *Bacillus bulgaricus* is still responsible for producing yogurt today. Few scientists now support a long life theory about yogurt, but there are many experiments to indicate that fermented milk can, in certain instances, have therapeutic benefits.

The French were calling yogurt 'lait de la vie eternelle' (milk of eternal life) long before Metchnikov put it under his microscope. This description dates from the sixteenth century, after a doctor from Constantinople gave goats' milk yogurt to the sick Emperor Francis I and produced a full recovery.

Long before that, fermented milk had a therapeutic reputation which modern research shows may not have been unfounded.

Cultured milks have been used and continue to be used in the treatment of stomach ulcers, colitis, gallbladder disorders, flatulence, constipation, diarrhoea, dysentery, and various intestinal disorders.

The lactic acid in yogurt does similar work in breaking down mild sugars as that normally done by our digestive juices. Fermented milk is partly pre-digested. This makes it a very useful food for ill and elderly persons, and for persons who have digestive or intestinal disorders or poor lactose tolerance.

The *Journal of the American Medical Association* carried an editorial under the heading 'A Funny Thing Happened On the Way to Get Some Yogurt', and mentioned experiments performed at the Rockefeller Institute. One group of mice had intestinal tracts exhibiting normal bacteria; a second group was fed so that *lactobactilli* were in the mice's intestines. The latter group, the 'yogurt mice', showed increased resistance to infections and poisons, lower infant deaths, and put on weight.

The *Medical World News* for 28 September 1962 reported experiments carried out by the Scientific Research Institute for Anticancer Antibodies of the Bulgarian Academy of Sciences, in which 136 out of 455 laboratory mice recovered from one kind of cancer tumour. All the mice had been injected with yogurt bacteria. Others with *lactobacilli* showed immunity to cancers.

Doctors have been puzzled by the low blood cholesterol levels of the Masai, an African tribe whose diet consists almost entirely of meat, blood, and milk, mostly soured. Despite their huge consumption of animal fats, the Masai are free of heart and artery diseases. Why?

Dr George V. Mann, of the Vanderbilt University School of Medicine may have hit upon the answer while testing the effects on the human body of a chemical additive used in manufacturing ice cream, mayonnaise, and some bakery products in the USA. He fed the additive to twelve Masai men in one gallon of yogurt a day, representing up to six hundred milligrams of cholesterol a day.

Dr Mann was surprised on examining the men's blood after three weeks to find their blood cholesterol levels had *fallen* during the massive consumption of yogurt. He concluded that consuming yogurt had somehow checked the normal daily production of cholesterol by the liver.

How important are the bacteria in fermented milk? Are they great fighters on our behalf – 'good' bacteria able to overcome 'bad' bacteria? I have mentioned some experiments – there are others – favourable to the 'friendly bacilli' idea. As so often in dietary investigation, the evidence is sometimes conflicting. Though there is no evidence to support the presence of a 'long life bacillus' in acid milks, it would seem that yogurt does have some therapeutic value.

One thing is certain: yogurt and other cultured milk contains all the natural goodness of the milk from which it is made. More: yogurt's content of protein, calcium, Vitamin B1 and B2 is higher that that of ordinary milk. If the yogurt is unsweetened, there are fewer calories than in sweet milk, especially if the low-fat kind is purchased or made at home using skimmed milk powder.

Nutrients in natural yogurt per 100 grams ($3\frac{1}{2}$ oz):

calories	57	Vitamin B2 (riboflavin)	·19 milligrams
protein	3·6 grams		
fat	2·6 grams	nicotinic acid (niacin)	·1 milligrams
carbohydrate	5·2 grams		
Vitamin B1 (thiamine)	·05 milligrams	calcium	140 milligrams
		iron	·1 milligrams

Yogurt also supplies Vitamins C, D, and E, others of the B group, and generous amounts of potassium and phosphorus.

There is nothing to beat home made yogurt and the method is well worth learning. Buy a carton of what you know to be good plain natural unsweetened yogurt, and use some of it to start making your own.

Homemade yogurt

A pint of whole, skimmed, or any other kind of milk makes a pint of yogurt. Experiment will reveal the amount of live culture to mix with the milk to produce the consistency you require. Most recipes give one or two tablespoonfuls per pint of milk.

Stage 1   Bring one pint (600 ml) of milk to the boil, which kills off unwanted bacteria.

Stage 2   Pour into a bowl and allow to cool to a temperature of about 43 °C (110 °F), a little above body temperature and just bearable for keeping your finger in a few seconds. You may like to add a tablespoonful or two of skimmed milk powder, for an additional concentration of nutrients. The cooling down process may be speeded up by putting the bowl in cold water.

Stage 3   Now stir in 1–2 tablespoons of the live plain yogurt. Mix well with a fork.

Stage 4   Pour the mixture into a wide-mouthed vacuum jar which has been rinsed out with warm water. Cover and leave undisturbed for about ten hours. If not using a vacuum flask, cover the bowl containing the mixed milk/yogurt mixture and leave undisturbed in a warm place for up to ten hours. The desired consistency may be obtained earlier. The point is for the mixture to remain at the same temperature all those hours, and therein lies any problem in making yogurt at home. Yogurt's bacteria thrives at the temperature mentioned. An electric oven at the lowest setting usually works. The top of your central heating boiler might do, or a warm airing cupboard. Covering the bowl with a blanket can help a lot. Ruth Bircher in her *Eating Your Way to Health* recommends 'a padded hay box', leaving the milk for twenty-four hours. Electric, thermostat-controlled yogurt-making machines are available for people wishing to speed up the process or who cannot achieve consistent results.

Stage 5   Refrigerate the yogurt for use as required. Remember to keep a tablespoonful or two for making your next lot.

Yogurt is delicious to eat by itself, and with fruit and muesli or other cereal. If you wish to add fruit juice or other natural flavouring, do so just before eating. Using flavoured yogurt as live culture does not usually work out well.

Yogurt can have many uses in preparing meals. The Russians put it in beetroot soup (*borsch*), and in Syria a yogurt soup called *shorbasi* is well liked; one version is made with white stock, flour, mint, butter, yogurt and paprika. The white stock contains veal, lemon, peppercorns, onion, white celery, and sage.

Yogurt makes a good ingredient for a salad dressing, or for a sauce. Chopped herbs can be mixed with the yogurt. Yogurt and parsley makes a simple but pleasant sauce.

Here is a Middle Eastern yogurt sauce.

Chachik

1 pint (600 ml) yogurt
1 large cucumber
2 tablespoons (30 ml) tarra-
  gon or wine vinegar
salt to taste

2½ oz (30 ml) cold water
2 cloves crushed garlic
2 tablespoons (30 ml) olive
  oil

Peel and finely chop the cucumber. Salt and leave for several minutes. Mix the yogurt and water and whisk until slightly frothy. Add the crushed garlic, cucumber, olive oil, and vinegar. Whisk well and serve cold.

Note that yogurt may be heated in cooking, but should not be brought to the boil, which causes it to curdle.

Kefir

This is another yogurt or yogurt-type fermented milk. I have given it a separate heading because *kefir* grains are sold in some health food shops.

Moslems call *kefir* the 'drink of the Prophet' and the dried pellets they use as culture they call 'drink grains of the Prophet'.

The name *kefir* probably derives from the Turkish '*keif*' meaning 'feeling good'. Moslem physicians for many centuries have used *kefir* for the treatment of dysentery and disorders of the intestinal tract.

Kefir is made by adding to sweet milk the dried 'grains' from a previous preparation. The grains can be kept to be used when the temperature is right for the bacilli to multiply. This unusual method of preparation is thought to have originated from the traditional use of leather pouches as containers for the milk. After use, 'grains' of dried *kefir* stuck to the sides and bottom of the pouches and when these were picked off it was found they could still act effectively as a culture.

Cheese

As milk sours its protein coagulates into *curd* which floats on top of the liquid *whey*. Like Miss Muffet, you can eat the curds and whey, but more often the curds are used to make cheese. Making cheese has a recorded history going back over six thousand years.

Cheese contains all the natural goodness of milk, but is more concentrated due to the considerable reduction in water content. Cow's milk is eighty-seven per cent water, Cheddar cheese is thirty-seven per cent water.

When looking to your daily protein supply, cheese should always be considered, especially by the lacto-vegetarian. Most cheeses supply a little more protein than meat and poultry, both by proportion of weight and by actual usability of protein in the body. The fat content is also high, which means that cheese should always be chewed well before it is swallowed. (Grating makes digestion easier.)

Cheddar cheese, which is a firm favourite in both Britain and America, is one of the most nutritious. Nutrients in 100 grams:

calories	412	Vitamin B1 (thiamine)	·04 milligrams
protein	25·4 grams		
fat	34·5 grams	Vitamin B2 (riboflavin)	·50 milligrams
carbohydrate	0		
Vitamin A	1050 i.u.	calcium	810 milligrams
		iron	·6 milligrams

Note the very high calcium content. Other nutrients are those found in milk.

A simple cheese can be made by placing soured skimmed milk in a muslin bag and hanging it so that the clear liquid whey can drip. When the dripping stops, you are left with a bagful of cheese. Most cheeses require more skill and attention than this in their preparation though, and home-cheese-production is not practical for most people.

There are more than four hundred varieties of cheese, and the milk used may come from the cow, goat, ewe, or other animals. In some cases milk from different animals is mixed to make the cheese.

The type of milk used has a bearing on the flavour of the cheese, as do other factors, such as the ripening time. Rennet may be used to coagulate the milk; this is an enzyme usually obtained from a calf's stomach.

The holes that are in some cheeses are caused by bacteria producing a gas that is trapped in the curd.

Roquefort is an example of the finesse that may be brought to cheesemaking. Ewe's milk is used, and it has to be just the right mixture of milk obtained in the morning and in the evening, at lambing time. Part of its special flavour is contributed by bread-crumbs that are allowed to develop a green mould and are then crushed. Finally the semi-hard, blue-veined Roquefort is stored in cool limestone caves. Other blue cheeses are *Danish Blue*, *Gorgon-zola*, and *Stilton*. *Stilton* is made from full-cream milk.

There are soft cheeses and hard cheeses. *Cheddar* is a hard cheese which grates well for use in cooking. *Parmesan* is another hard cheese, and is traditionally grated on to cooked spaghetti.

Cottage cheese is soft and unripened, with a large- or small-curd texture. It has more than double the water content of Cheddar and much fewer calories. Slimmers should however make sure they get the variety that is uncreamed, made from skimmed milk, and low in fat.

Those who dislike the often granular and sticky texture of cottage cheese are unlikely to be disappointed with the French *fromage frais* (fresh cheese), which can also be low-fat but which has the consistency and texture of thick yogurt. It is made from cows' or goats' milk and lends itself to many culinary uses.

Cottage cheese is an acid curd cheese made from pasteurised defatted milk. Lactic-acid bacteria sour the milk. Rennet and slow heat coagulate the milk's protein (casein) into a soft curd, which is cut and drained of whey. The curd is washed in cold water and is then ready to eat.

The cheeses first made thousands of years ago were probably sour-milk cheeses. It was soon found that by draining off the watery whey a fresh acid-curd cheese remained. Simple fresh cheeses are still made in farm cottages in many countries such as the German Handkäse ('hand-made cheeses').

Cream cheeses are made from double cream, adding considerably to the fat and calorie content. Cottage cheese is low in fat and high in protein; the reverse is true of cream cheese. The following figures are for 100 grams:

	Calories	Protein g	Fat f	Calcium mg
Cottage cheese	113	19·5	3·9	81
Cream cheese	813	3·3	86	30

Cottage cheese is not ripened, but most other cheeses are ripened for anything from three to sixteen months. But once purchased, it should be used fairly quickly as it can 'go off'.

Nutritious Nuts

A strange thing about nuts – some of the best-known ain't! I don't just mean that they are seeds: plant them in the right soil and they will germinate and grow. Grains, beans, and peas are also seeds. What I mean is, for example, that the almond is really a drupe, a stone fruit, like a peach or a plum; the Brazil nut is really a seed; and the popular peanut is really a legume, a family of plants that includes beans and peas. But common classification and usage will be good enough for us here.

What is certain is that nuts should not be food only for squirrels, or even only for vegetarians. They should be a regular part of every person's diet who gives some thought to natural nutrition. Here nature has concentrated extraordinary nutritive power. Nuts are generally low in water, high in energy (calories), and vegetable protein, extremely high in fatty acids, high in fibre, and rich in vitamins, minerals, and trace minerals.

Concentrated value

When a food is low in water content there is usually a good concentration of whatever nutrients it has to give.

To look at the water content of some common foods:

raw cabbage	92 per cent	cod	66 per cent
broad beans	90 per cent	roast lamb	58 per cent
cows' milk	87 per cent	wholewheat	36 per cent
boiled potatoes	80 per cent	bread	
egg	74 per cent	dried apricots	25 per cent
		dried figs	23 per cent

What percentage of water in nuts?
Almonds 5 per cent,
Roast peanuts 2 per cent.

But the coconut, as in other respects, is the joker in the pack,
having 55 per cent water even when desiccated (dried).

Nuts for energy

The meagre water content and high amounts of protein and especially fats in nuts, plus some carbohydrate, give them very high
energy ratings. Food's fuel power is measured in calories or joules.
Calories and joules are not nutrients, but are units of measurement
of the heat/energy a food produces when metabolised in the body.
Weight for weight, the energy value of nuts is greatly superior to
that of such animal protein foods as meat, poultry and fish.

Energy value in calories per 100 grams:

Brazil nuts, unsalted	680	pork, average	408
pecans, raw, halves	680	lamb, roast	284
walnuts, English, raw	650	beef, average	313
cashews, unsalted	590	egg, fresh	158
peanuts, roasted	586	cod, haddock	69
almonds	580		
bacon, average	476		

Nuts for protein

Nuts are a major source of protein for vegetarians, and especially for vegans who do not eat egg, milk, or cheese. There is no problem in getting enough protein from nuts and pulses, though vegetable protein foods do need to be combined at a meal, to 'complete' their amino acids either with another vegetable protein or with an animal protein. Nearly all vegetable protein foods supply a healthier type of fat than that of the animal protein foods. Consumers of animal foods need to counterbalance their saturated fat with the un-saturated fat of the vegetable protein foods, of which nuts are a prime example.

Let us look at the protein content of nuts and animal protein foods in grams per 100 grams:

chickens, roast	29·6	cashews	18·0
beef, stewed steak	29·0	Brazil nuts	15·0
peanuts, roasted	28·1	walnuts, English	14·0
cheese, cheddar	25·4	pork, average	12·0
walnuts, black	20·5	egg, fresh	11·9
almonds	20·5	pecans	10·0

Nuts and seeds have a protein usability of forty-five to fifty-five per cent compared with sixty-seven per cent for meats and poultry, but in terms of food value nuts must be considered a very useful source of protein in the human diet, a source that deserves to be better known.

Jon Wynne-Tyson, put the case for vegetarianism passionately in *Food For A Future*, when he wrote:

'The fact of the matter is that nuts are an excellent source of nutrition and one that has been almost totally disregarded in a society determined to centre its eating on meat rather than on the foods for which our species is specifically constructed and chemically attuned. Nuts almost more than any other made-for-man as distinct from man-made food put the five-pounds-of-lentil-porridge school to flight, their high nutritive value making it unnecessary that they be eaten in such large quantities as the watery meats.

Beans and pulses, hardly less neglected in the West, also help greatly to achieve an easier and more natural balance of nutrients, reducing the total food intake with all the extra mental and physical alertness this invariably brings.'

Dr Frank Wokes, in *Plant Foods For Human Nutrition*, vol. 1, no. 1, May 1968 wrote:

'Although animal foods are generally considered to be richer sources of protein, various plant foods such as nuts and pulses have a higher protein content than meat, milk or eggs calculated either on their composition as prepared for cooking or eating, or on the calorie basis. Deficiency of some essential amino acids such as lysine or methionine in individual plant proteins can be largely overcome by blending different plant proteins producing mixtures with biological values perhaps 15–25 per cent below those of human milk protein.'

The best is got out of nuts' protein in a *muesli* composed of whole grains, wheat germ, bran, nuts, fruit, and milk or cream. Milk or cheese also 'complete' nut protein – the phosphorus in the nuts working well with the calcium in milk or cheese. Nuts, beans and seeds combine to supply good protein too; try a mix of peanuts, soy beans, and sesame seeds.

Nuts for fats

Foods containing fats are usually a combination of both saturated and unsaturated fats, often with one or the other predominating. Saturated fats are hard at room temperature, and unsaturated fats soft or liquid. Saturated fats are found mostly in animal solid fats e.g. meats, egg yolk, milk, cream, cheese, and butter. A diet high in saturated fats may cause a dangerous build up of cholesterol deposits on the walls of the arteries. Foods high in the soft or liquid unsaturated fats are usually vegetable (with the exception of ordinary margarines), and most nuts have a high fat content that is strongly unsaturated. More about the importance of unsaturated fats in the diet will be given when we discuss seed and plant oils in Chapter 9.

Saturated and unsaturated fats per 100 grams edible portion:

	Total grams saturated fatty acids	*Total grams unsaturated fatty acids*
beef	12	12
lamb	12	9
pork	19	27
chicken	2	3
cows' milk	15	10
cheese, cheddar	18	12
cheese, cream	21	13
eggs, hens'	4	6
herring	2	2
butter	46	29
margarine, ordinary	18–19	60–61
wheatgerm	2	8
olive oil	11	83
safflower oil	8	87
soya bean oil	15	72
olives	2	16
sesame seed, whole	7	40
almonds	4	47
Brazil nuts	13	49
cashews	8	35
coconut	30	2
peanut	10	34
pecan	5	59
walnut, black	4	49

(Watts, B. K., Merrill, A. L., *Composition of Foods*, US Department of Agriculture, 1963.)

Macadamia nuts, pecans, and black walnuts have more than 70 per cent fat, Brazil nuts and hazelnuts (filberts), more than 60 per cent, and almonds more than 50 per cent.

Carbohydrate

Most nuts supply similar amounts of carbohydrate to their protein content, in some cases equal it, and in the case of cashews, chestnuts, and coconuts well exceed it. Carbohydrates supply heat and energy, and in the average diet come from cereals, bread, pastas, potatoes, sugar, honey, and other sweeteners.

Vitamins and minerals

Nuts are generally well supplied with the B vitamins, especially Vitamin B3 (nicotinic acid, niacin). Almonds, hazelnuts, and peanuts contain Vitamin E. As seeds, with the potential of germination and growth, nuts are rich in minerals, especially iron and phosphorus, and also supply calcium, potassium, and magnesium in good measure and many trace minerals.

Fibre

Nuts provide a good contribution of fibre, whose importance for the modern diet was explained on p. 61. Coconut supplies 4 grams per 100 grams of edible portion, Brazil nuts 3 grams, almonds 2·6 grams, peanuts 2·4 grams, and pecans 2·1 grams.

Almonds

The 'divine fruit' to the ancient Hebrews. Almonds are the kernels of stone-fruits borne by two trees related to the plum and peach, which makes them, botanically, a drupe or droop rather than a nut. Originally native to Central and Western Asia, they are now grown commercially in Mediterranean Europe, particularly Italy and Spain, and in California. Jordan almonds, despite their name, are grown in the countryside around Malaga.

There are two general types of almond: the inedible bitter almond and the edible sweet almond. The former contains the poison prussic acid, which manufacturers extract; the remaining almond oil being used as a flavouring agent and in the manufacture of cosmetics.

It is the sweet edible almond that concerns us. 100 grams of sweet almonds supply 580 calories of energy, 20·5 grams of protein, 4·3 grams of carbohydrate, and 53·5 grams of fat, which includes about 11 grams of linoleic acid, a key essential fatty acid which is important in the control of cholesterol in the body. Raw almonds also supply the B vitamins, Vitamin E (14 mg in 100 g), calcium, iron, phosphorus, potassium, magnesium, copper, manganese and selenium. They also provide 2·6 grams of fibre in every 100 grams.

Sweet almonds are versatile in their use. They can be blanched, roasted, fried, salted, sugared, and ground. They may be used in soups, salads, savouries, meat and fish dishes, sweets and desserts. They are used as flavouring and decoration in cakes, pastries, and biscuits. They are important to the skills of the French pâtissiers, and the Italians make considerable use of almonds in their recipes.

The Arabs like nutty sweetmeats made from almonds, such as nougat, which they introduced into Europe in the Middle Ages when huge quantities of almonds were consumed by wealthy families. In those days almond 'milk' was often substituted for cows' milk. It is particularly easy to digest, and supplies good vegetable protein.

Almond 'Milk'

1½ tablespoons skinned sweet almonds

1 teaspoon honey
¾ cup (6 oz) water

Mix in mixer or electric liquidiser. Strain if necessary.

Women who are pregnant or breast-feeding should note that some writers on nutrition say that almonds and almond 'milk' stimulate milk secretion.

Cheese and almonds go well together, both for taste and for nutrition. The amino acids in the cheese complement those in the almonds and the calcium in the cheese works well with the phosphorus in the almonds.

Brazil nuts (para or cream nuts)

The seed of the *Berholettia excelsa*, a myrtaceous tree of Brazil. Really a seed rather than a true nut, but for all practical purposes a superb dessert nut that can also be chopped or ground for cooking.

The fruit of the tree is large and spherical, weighing several pounds. Inside the fruit the nuts cling together like the segments of an orange. The seed, inside the hard three-sided shell, is plump with a creamy texture and taste.

Brazil nuts are grown chiefly in South America. There is concentrated richness in raw Brazil nuts. 100 grams contain 14 grams of protein and more than 60 grams of fat, including 17 grams of linoleic acid, ·90 milligrams of Vitamin B1, 1·8 milligrams of nicotinic acid (niacin), and 7 milligrams of Vitamin E. There is a full range of minerals typical of nuts, and the fuel power is 650 calories.

Cashews

The rich kidney-shaped nut of the tropical tree, *Anacardium Occidentale*, once native to Brazil but now grown throughout South America. They are roasted to remove a fluid in the shell that irritates the skin. The kernel, when released, is sweet tasting and has the highest rating among nuts for making its protein available, nearly 60 per cent.

Chestnuts

The large, reddish-brown nut of the chestnut tree *Castanea vesca*, (not the inedible horse chestnut). The sweet Spanish chestnut is widely grown in southern Europe, to which it is native. The fattest and best for cooking come from France, Italy, and Spain.

The sweet chestnut is, like the coconut, something of a nut oddity. It is high in moisture and in starchy carbohydrate (more than forty per cent), and has only two per cent each of protein and fat.

Because of its starch, it can be cooked like a vegetable. Its floury texture blends well with poultry and game, as well as other meats.

To roast: slit the pointed ends with a sharp knife and roast under a hot grill or in an oven at moderate setting, but the traditional method is in front of an open fire. When ready to eat the shells split open. There are still hot chestnut vendors, complete with burning brazier, on city streets in Britain and in other countries.

To cook: blanch in boiling water and peel. Cover again in boiling water and simmer for 45–60 minutes.

Coconut

Something of a freak among nuts. The fruit of the tropical palm, *Cocusnucifera*. Inside the large, hard, fibrous, brown husk is an edible white lining and a pale liquid that can be drunk. The solid oil obtained from the white lining is used in making soap, candles and ointment. Oil is also extracted for use as cooking oil and to make margarine.

Don't expect unsaturated fats from coconut oil, margarine, or the raw 'meat'. The coconut is untypical of nuts in having predominantly saturated fats. In 100 grams there are 24·3 grams of saturated fat and only 2 grams of unsaturated fat, and, so artificial milk products made from coconut are not suitable for anyone cutting down on saturated fat.

The milk is easily digested and the 'meat' contains oils, B vitamins, and minerals.

The meat has a high water content, 55 per cent, even when dried out (desiccated), and has nearly three times more carbohydrate than protein. 100 grams of fresh shredded coconut flesh contain 340 calories, 9 grams carbohydrate, 3·15 grams protein, 35·2 grams of fat, 3·4 grams of fibre, and 1·7 milligrams of iron.

Hazelnuts and filberts

The fruit of the small hazel or cob nut tree. The nuts grow wild in many parts of Europe, North America, the Middle East, and Asia, and are grown commercially in Europe and in America. The best hazels come from Spain, Italy and Turkey. The country at Avellino, behind Naples, has the reputation of producing the finest hazels and gave the hazel tree its botanical name *Corylus avellana*.

The French filberts, from the related *Corylus maxima*, are named after St Philibert, a seventh-century Norman. The nuts are ripe about St Philibert's Day, 22 August. The Kentish cob is a filbert.

Hazels have a bitter-tasting brown inside skin that needs removing. The skins peel off if the nuts are grilled in a moderate oven for 10–15 minutes. The peeled nuts can be eaten raw, roasted, or ground. They can be used for nut roasts and as an accompaniment to savoury dishes. They may also be used in puddings, cakes, and confectionery. They are pleasant to eat when baked in an oven until a light golden brown.

Their outstanding nutritional feature is their high content of unsaturated fatty acids. In 100 grams there are 59 grams of unsaturated fatty acids and 4·2 grams of saturated fatty acids.

Macadamia nuts

A nut that is a native of Australia, and becoming popular in the United States. Its fat content is over seventy per cent and it contains over nine per cent protein. It supplies 109 calories in 15 grams, about six average nuts.

Peanuts

Known also as ground nuts, earth nuts, monkey nuts, goobers, and pinders. Peanuts are inexpensive, plentiful, and plebian – but there is nothing inferior about their nutritional status!

Peanuts are the pods of a leguminous plant, which relates them, botanically, to peas and beans. Their method of growth is unusual, growing on a small bushy plant, and having to be harvested from the ground. After the plant's flowers have been pollinated, the stalks bend to the ground and extend to push the pods into the soil, where they mature. There are two to four nuts in each shell, which is easily opened with the fingers.

Peanuts were a favourite food of the Incas but were eaten in Peru before the Incas. The Incas buried a container of peanuts alongside their dead, and those that have been dug up in recent times often have been good enough to eat or to plant. The Peruvians called the plant *mani* or ground seed.

Though native to South America, the peanut plant is now cultivated in many parts of the world. It is one of the most nutritious nuts, having a high content of unsaturated fatty acids, protein, vitamins, and minerals.

Nutrients in 100 grams of roasted peanuts:

calories	586	nicotinic acid	16 milligrams
protein	28·1 grams	(niacin)	
fat	49·0 grams	calcium	61 milligrams
carbohydrate	8·6 grams	iron	2 milligrams
Vitamin B1	·23 milligrams	phosphorus	400 milligrams
(thiamine)		potassium	674 milligrams
Vitamin B2	·10 milligrams		
(riboflavin)			

There are 14 grams of linoleic acid in the fat. That 28·1 grams of protein is more weight for weight than the protein content of beef, pork, lamb, cod, haddock, and Cheddar cheese. Peanuts are cholesterol free and unsaturated fats predominate, 50 grams to 15 grams of saturated fat.

The nuts can be added to a variety of dishes. They are used for the manufacture of peanut oil, which has a high scorching point and is good for deep frying. It makes a neutral salad dressing. Peanut butter is worthy of regular inclusion in the diet, proving a good measure of nutrients. The Americans eat half a billion pounds of it in a year. Buy the kind that is unsweetened and salted with sea salt. You can make your own, using a mill or a blender. To each cup of peanuts add 1½ to 2½ cups of vegetable oil – safflower is particularly good. Salt with sea salt.

Pecans

Neatly-described as 'walnuts with zippers', the pecan is a rich nut that deserves to be as well known in Europe as it is in the US. It comes from a tree that is a member of the *Carya* family and is native to North America. Large crops are cultivated in Texas and Oklahoma.

The pecan's uses in cooking are similar to those for the walnut. The Americans put them in pies and flans.

100 grams of raw pecans supply 683 calories, 9·1 grams protein, 14·5 grams carbohydrate, 72 grams fat, 2·1 grams fibre, ·86 milligrams Vitamin B1, ·13 milligrams Vitamin B2, some nicotinic acid (niacin), Vitamin A, Vitamin E, pantothenic acid, Vitamin C, iron (2·4 milligrams), calcium, phosphorus, magnesium, and other minerals. Its unsaturated fatty acids loom over the saturated to the ratio 63:5.

Pine nuts or kernels

The seeds of the cone of the Stone Pine, useful in protein, about thirteen per cent, and with about fifty per cent fat. Its taste is similar to the almond. It is cultivated in the USA, Mexico, Asia and the Mediterranean.

The nutrients in the raw nuts are impressive. In addition to the 13 grams of protein and the 50 grams of fat already mentioned, 100 grams also supply 1·26 milligrams Vitamin B1, ·24 milligrams

Vitamin B2, 4·6 milligrams nicotinic acid (niacin), and 4·85 milligrams iron.

Pine nuts may be used to make nut milk as for almonds.

Pistachio nuts

The nut of the *Pistacia vera*, grown in the US, Mexico, Iran,
Afghanistan, Syria and Italy.

They have been found on archaeological sites in the Near East
showing that people were eating them about 10000 BC.

The skin is yellow and wrinkled, and breaks open easily to reveal the small bright green kernel which has a distinctive sweet
taste as attractive as its colour.

It can be eaten as a dessert nut, but also goes well with savoury
dishes, and can be used in cakes and desserts. They are particularly tasty with ice cream. 100 grams contain 18 grams protein and
50 grams fat with a saturated/unsaturated ratio of 1:6. They also
supply a good measure of the B vitamins, 6·6 milligrams iron, and
other minerals associated with nuts.

Walnuts

The fruit of the walnut tree, *Juglans regia*. The English walnut has
a delicate flavour. The black walnut, *Juglans nigra*, has a stronger
flavour.

Pickled walnuts are made from the whole nut before the shell has
hardened and go well with cold meats or cheese.

Walnut oil may be used as a salad oil, if you like its distinctive
flavour.

Its nutrient content is impressive. Walnuts have more polyunsaturated fatty acids than saturated fatty acids.

100 grams of English walnuts supply:

calories	651	Vitamin B1	·33 milligrams
protein	14·8 grams	(thiamine)	
carbohydrate	15·8 grams	Vitamin B2	·13 milligrams
saturated fat	4·5 grams	(riboflavin)	
unsaturated fat	49·5 grams	Vitamin B6	·73 milligrams
fibre	2·1 grams	biotin	37 mcg
		folic acid	·066 milligrams

nicotinic acid 1·9 milligrams   calcium   99 milligrams
  (niacin)   iron   3·1 milligrams

Walnuts also contain some of the Vitamins A, C, and E, and the minerals phosphorus, potassium, magnesium, copper, manganese and zinc.

Storage

For freshness and to retain full nutrient worth, nuts should be kept in their shells until immediately before use. Shelled nuts should be kept in an airtight container and stored in a cool dry place. As the oils in nuts start turning rancid soon after being exposed to air chopped or ground nuts should be used quickly.

All kinds of nuts will keep moist and fresh when frozen, either whole or chopped, but should not be salted (an unhealthy practice, anyway). They will keep for up to a year in a freezer, in small containers, foil, or polythene bags.

Digestibility

Whole nuts should be chewed well for good digestion. Chopping and grating them and mixing them with other foods will assist any person who finds whole nuts difficult to digest.

Incidentally, chewing nuts is excellent exercise for the face muscles, a neglected part of the body in the matter of exercise. Facial muscles benefit from exercise just as readily as arms and legs, improving firmness, tone, and contour. I wasn't simply being facetious when I included chewing peanuts as an exercise in my book *New Faces* (A. Thomas).

Uses

Full nutrient benefit is obtained from raw nuts, if possible, straight from the shell; but their culinary uses need not be foregone.

With their rich content of fats, protein, B vitamins, iron, calcium, and other minerals, nuts add nutrients as well as texture and piquancy to vegetable and rice dishes, and to salads. Chinese cooks make good use of walnuts and cashews in their vegetable dishes. Nuts also go well with grains and dried fruit. With grains there is a good build up of vegetable proteins. Nuts and dried fruits can be added to a *muesli* for one of the most complete foods possible. They also make a nutritious snack in themselves. Indeed, nuts are the ideal snack food, and nuts, seeds, and dried fruits are often found in the kind of snack bars sold in health food shops. Peanuts and raisins make a simple and inexpensive snack.

Nuts may also be added to soups, cakes, and biscuits, or used to make nut butters, nut 'milks', nut roasts, nut rissoles, and meat substitutes.

Nut Rissoles

Mix together peanuts, onion, garlic, herbs, seasoning, and mashed lentils.

Bind with a beaten egg, and shape as required.

Coat with breadcrumbs and fry in a vegetable oil.

Nut butters can be made by grinding nuts and mixing them with vegetable oil and a little sea salt. Safflower makes a good oil for this purpose. Health food shops sell almond, cashew, peanut and other 'butters'. They can be used as a spread for bread and biscuits, put in soups and stews, mixed with a cream cheese, and so on.

When planning dishes, note that broccoli and cauliflower go particularly well with nuts; so do peas and most beans. Remember, too, that milk, yogurt, and cheese balance and complete the proteins in nuts and seeds and that combinations of nuts, beans, and seeds provide excellent protein.

Great Little Seeds

Seed power

'And God said, "Behold, I have given you every herb bearing seed, which *is* upon the face of all the earth, and every tree, in which *is* the fruit of a tree yielding seed; to you it shall be for meat".' (Genesis 1:29).

Mankind has been eating seeds since time immemorial. Human life has at times been sustained by little or nothing other than seeds, and the proliferation of seeds and plants does not disturb us as does the proliferation of insect and animal life. Seeds are our sustenance and our greater potential sustenance. It is staggering to contemplate that each seed we eat is a potential plant, and that each seed contains all the nutrients necessary for producing a plant. Seeds provide protein, fats, carbohydrate, vitamins, minerals, fibre, and water – all the elements for natural nutrition.

The power of the seed is startling. Rutherford Platt writes in *The Great American Forest*:

'In 1875, a Massachusetts farmer, curious about the growing power of expanding apples, melons and squashes, harnessed a squash to a weight-lifting device which had a dial like a grocer's scale to indicate the pressure exerted by the expanding fruit. As the days passed, he kept piling on counterbalancing weight; he could hardly believe his eyes when he saw his vegetables quietly exerting a lifting force of five thousand pounds per square inch. When nobody believed him, he set up exhibits of harnessed squashes and invited the public to come and see. The *Annual Report of the Massachusetts Board of Agriculture*, 1875, reported: "Many thousands of men, women, and children of all classes of society visited it. Mr Penlow watched it day and night, making hourly observations; Professor Parker was moved to write a poem about it; Professor Seelye declared that he positively stood in awe of it."'

A tree root can cleave a one-and-a-half ton boulder, or shatter a pavement slabstone. All this power is concentrated at first in a little seed.

But it is seeds' nutritive power that concerns us here, and while grains are seeds, nuts are seeds, beans are seeds, and there are seeds in vegetables and in fruits, this chapter is reserved for some great little seeds that qualify as health foods. In particular, I have in mind sunflower, safflower, and sesame seeds, and as these are noted for their oils, this chapter seems a good place to include plant oils. (Those of sunflower, safflower, and sesame top the table for their healthful fatty acids.) It seems the right juncture, too, for saying more about the composition and importance of fats and in particular of essential fatty acids, mentioned in Chapter 8 when discussing nuts.

Why we need fats

Fats provide the greatest concentration of fuel power for the body, more that double that supplied by the same weight of either protein or carbohydrate. One gram of fat supplies heat/energy measuring nine calories. One gram of either protein or carbohydrate supplies four calories. (Strictly, these figures refer to Calories, i.e. large calories, but it is customary in writing about diet to use the lower case 'c'. The Calorie is one thousand times greater than the calorie, and is the amount of heat required to raise the temperature of 1 kg (1000 g) of water through 1 °C. The calorie is being replaced in use by the joule, the unit of energy in the metric system. 1 calorie = 4·2 joules (J) and 1 Calorie = 4·2 kilojoules (kJ).)

What else are fats needed for? Here are some answers:

To carry the fat soluble Vitamins A, D, E, and K.

To satisfy the appetite by giving a feeling of fullness and satisfaction after a meal.

To heat insulate the body and preserve body heat.

To hold in place and cushion the internal organs.

To improve the flavour of foods. Fats acts as a solvent for food flavours.

To stimulate the bile flow.

To coat the nerves protectively (the myelin sheath).

To provide an intestinal lubricant that helps the elimination of waste.

To provide the essential fatty acids (EFA) which are needed for certain vital physiological functions. These can only be obtained from fat in the diet.

Saturated and unsaturated fats

There is no question of not needing fat in your diet. The only question is, what kind of fat – saturated or unsaturated? Foods contain a mixture of both, but the balance of these is crucial.

In *saturated fats* each carbon atom combines with two hydrogen atoms, except for the terminal carbon atoms. This produces a fat that is solid at room temperature – the kind found in meat, lard, suet, butter, cream, and cheese.

The *unsaturated fats* are composed of polyunsaturated fats and monounsaturated fats and have only some of their atoms or molecules joined with hydrogen; they tend to be soft or liquid at room temperature.

Animal fats tend to be high in *cholesterol*, a white waxy alcohol. Cholesterol is no enemy in itself, and our livers manufacture it, to supply our brains and nervous systems. It has other important functions to perform, including some connected with the absorption of fat in the intestines. The reason so much publicity has been given to the dangers of cholesterol is that an excessive build up in the blood (high blood cholesterol), if not cleared, often leads to deposits of fat on the walls of the arteries narrowing them. Blood clots may then develop, blocking the arteries and causing a heart attack (coronary thrombosis), one of the great modern killers.

The American Heart Association stated:

'The reduction or control of fat consumption under medical supervision, with reasonable substitution of polyunsaturated for saturated fats, is recommended as a possible means of preventing atherosclerosis and decreasing the risk of heart attacks and strokes.'

Polyunsaturated fats are liquid fats, such as safflower, sunflower, sesame, and soybean, and other vegetable oils. Oils high in poly-unsaturated oils are used in making cooking oils, salad dressings, and soft margarines.

Monounsaturated fats may be either hard or soft or a combina-tion of both. They are found in a variety of foods, both animal and vegetable. They have little, if any, effect on blood cholesterol levels.

Manufacturers make use of a process called *hydrogenation* to increase the shelf life of some fatty foods. The effect, as in ordinary margarines, is to harden and to partially saturate the food.

Essential fatty acids

Seeds, nuts, soybeans, and plant oils particularly are the best sources of the essential fatty acids – called 'essential' because they cannot be synthesised in the body and have to be obtained from the diet. The three most important are *linoleic* acid, *linolenic* acid, and *arachidonic* acid. The condition of the blood, arteries, and nerves depends on them. They are important, too, for the control of cholesterol.

Linoleic is a key fatty acid, for linolenic and arachidonic acids can be made from it. The National Research Council in America says that linoleic acid should provide about two per cent of the calories in the diet.

Linoleic acid in grams per 100 grams of edible portion:

safflower oil	72	sunflower seeds	30
(7 tablespoons)		sesame seeds	20
sunflower oil	65	peanuts and peanut	
(7 tablespoons)		butter	14
corn, cottonseed, peanut,		Brazil nuts	14
soybean oil (7		soy flour	10
tablespoons)	50	potatoes, fried in oil	8
sesame oil		soybeans	7
(7 tablespoons)	42	olive oil	7
walnuts, English	40	chicken, roast	4

The importance of seeds and seed oils for linoleic acid is now clear. Dr Michael Crawford, in *What We Eat Today*, in discussing the essential fatty acids, refers to 'the seed kind (linoleic) and the leafy kind (linolenic)'. He believes it is important to health to balance these two kinds of fatty acids. Monkeys given an unbalanced mixture of the two acids develop disease, which clears up when the balance is restored. Dr Crawford points out that as less fruit and vegetables are eaten today, so less essential fatty acids are obtained, and links this with increased heart disease.

Taking vegetable oils rich in linoleic acid promotes the breakdown of fats and cholesterol. One to two tablespoons of oil daily will be beneficial but not taken all at one time. The need will be less, the fewer saturated fats in your diet.

Research indicates that a full range of nutrients promotes a healthy body that makes efficient use of its fats and its cholesterol. The B vitamins, especially B1, choline, inositol, and B6, Vitamin E, and magnesium all play a part in keeping cholesterol in balance. Large doses (megadoses) of Vitamins A and C have been known to reduce blood cholesterol levels in heart patients. But once again it is a good overall diet that is most important. In planning such a diet the nutrient power of seeds should not be forgotten.

As we get older, we take longer to clear fats from the blood. The essential fatty acids, the phospholipid lecithin, the B vitamins, and Vitamin E all help in the utilisation of fats, which means that these nutrients are particularly important in middle and later life.

It should be noted that overdosing with polyunsaturated oils can upset the balance of health just as surely as not having enough. A baby died in America from a deficiency of Vitamin E after being overdosed with polyunsaturated fats. Doctors looked into the case and came up with the precise information that ·6 milligrams of Vitamin E is needed for every gram of unsaturated fat in the diet.

It is a matter of balance. We need saturated fats as well as unsaturated fats in our diet. Our cells are built from protein and fat, and about seventeen per cent of our body fat is unsaturated. This may be a clue to how to balance our fats. Few nutritionists and writers on eating for health are prepared to give a precise answer. An exception is Dr Carlton Fredericks, described by his publishers as 'America's best known nutritionist'. Writing in *Eating Right For You*, he says: 'I long ago set a figure of about 20 per cent unsaturated fat as a reasonable goal.'

Nutrients in seeds

In addition to the polyunsaturated oils, with their essential fatty acids, seeds, like sesame and sunflower, contain very useful amounts of protein, fibre, iron, calcium, phosphorus, potassium, trace minerals, the B vitamins and Vitamin E. Vitamin E is important for helping keep healthy the blood, blood vessels, and heart. Most seeds contain nitrilosides, which some researchers believe give protection against the formation of tumours.

Safflower seeds

The safflower is a tall composite plant, *Carthamus tinctorius*, which is allied to the thistle and yields a red dye that is used in rouge and by the Egyptians to dye silk. Oil from the seeds can provide as much as eighty-seven per cent unsaturated fat and is unsurpassed for its seventy-two per cent supply of linoleic acid, the key essential fatty acid. One tablespoon (14 grams) supplies 10·5 milligrams of Vitamin E. The bland, odourless oil is used as a salad oil and for cooking.

Sunflower seeds

The USA and the USSR are the world's leading exporters of the seeds of the sunflower, a plant of the genus *Helianthus*, named from the form and colour of its large flower, brown in the centre with yellow petals. Its face follows the sun's seeming movement through the day.

Viewed nutritionally, sunflower seeds seem a gift from the sun, being rich in protein (twenty-four per cent), unsaturated fats (fifty-two per cent, including thirty per cent linoleic acid), ten amino acids, natural enzymes, B group vitamins, calcium, iron, phosphorus, potassium, and such trace elements as copper, manganese, and zinc.

100 grams of sunflower seeds supplies:

calories	560	nicotinic acid	27·2 mg
protein	24 grams	(niacin)	
fat	52 grams	iron	7 mg
fibre	3·8 grams	calcium	120 mg
Vitamin B1	3·6 mg	phosphorus	836 mg
(thiamine)		potassium	920 mg
Vitamin B2	·4 mg		
(riboflavin)			

One tablespoon (14 grams) of sunflower oil supplies 1·3 milligrams of Vitamin E.

Sunflower seeds can be bought at health food stores, herbal shops, and some general stores. They can be chewed by themselves, mixed in a *muesli*, used for topping bread, sprinkled on yogurt, eaten with a salad, and so on.

You can also use the oil for salads, in mayonnaise, and for cooking.

What is left of the seeds after the oil has been crushed out is made into meal which is mostly fed to animals. Sunflower meal has hardly any fat, which went out with the oil, but contains 56·8 per cent protein and 5·9 per cent fibre, according to an analysis performed at Texas A & M University.

Sesame seeds

Sesame seeds provided oil for several ancient civilisations. The ancient Romans made copious use of it. Sesame oil appears in the earliest records of Africa and the Far East.

Whole sesame seeds are rich in protein, fats, Vitamins B1 and B2, nicotinic acid, and other B complex vitamins, iron, calcium, other minerals and trace elements. The seeds contain twenty per cent linoleic acid and the oil forty-two per cent. In 100 grams of the whole hulled seeds there are 18 grams of protein, 48 grams of fat, 10·4 milligrams of iron, and 110 milligrams of calcium. One tablespoon (14 grams) of sesame oil supplies 3·2 milligrams of Vitamin E.

Sesame seeds and sesame oil have similar uses to those for sunflower seeds and oil. The sesame seed spread *tahini* is popular in the Near East, and sold in health food shops in the West. You can make your own: mix ground seeds with water, lemon, sea salt, garlic, herbs, and so on, according to taste. Sesame seeds can be mixed with flour for making bread. You can use sesame purée, slightly diluted, with a *muesli*, or use it to make sesame milk or cream. Helva Purée is a commercial product. The milk or cream goes well with *muesli* and with cold fruit dishes.

Sesame Milk or Cream

1 tablespoon sesame purée (Helva Purée)
1 teaspoon honey

1 teaspoon lemon juice
1 cup (8 oz) water, cold or warm

Whisk the purée and honey together. Add water and lemon juice slowly.

Use less water to make cream.

Fresh fruit juice may be added to make Sesame Frappé.

Pumpkin and squash seeds

A superb vegetable protein and source of iron.
Nutrients in 100 grams, dried and hulled:

calories	553	Vitamin B2 (riboflavin)	·20 milligrams
protein	29 grams	nicotinic acid (niacin)	·102 milligrams
fat	46·7 grams	iron	11·2 milligrams
unsaturated fat	36·4 grams		
carbohydrate	3 grams	calcium	50 milligrams
Vitamin A	72 i.u.		
Vitamin B1 (thiamine)	·24 milligrams	phosphorus	1144 milligrams

Pumpkin seeds can be toasted or used as the other seeds mentioned above.

Hulling seeds is often a problem.

An American government agriculture research centre has managed to breed a pumpkin whose seeds do not have to be shucked. The seeds are hull-less – naked, though not in this case as nature intended. The name of the new breed of pumpkin is *Lady Godiva*.

There are other seeds of culinary and medicinal value, such as anise, caraway, poppy, and various herbs. Those discussed in this chapter have particular nutrient potency and are very good sources of poly-unsaturated oils.

Other vegetable oils

It is useful to vary the oils you use, for the content of the essential fatty acids (Vitamin F) varies, as we saw with linoleic acid. You can also mix oils for use, combining their proportions of fatty acids.

Corn, cottonseed, peanut, and soybean oils supply about 50 grams of linoleic acid in 100 grams. Olive oil has only seven per cent linoleic acid, but is rich in oleic acid which aids digestibility. As olives are easy to press, the oil is obtained without processing and retains its flavour. As in ancient times, it is the Mediterranean countries – Greece, Italy, and Spain – that mainly produce it, and where it is used as a salad and cooking oil. The lowish content of linoleic acid can be corrected by mixing olive oil with safflower oil, which has the highest content of linoleic acid.

The two other main essential fatty acids, linolenic and arachidonic, are well supplied by soybean oil and peanut oil respectively.

Corn oil provides useful amounts of the essential fatty acids and 78 milligrams of Vitamin E in 100 grams of oil, a figure higher than that of any other oil except wheat germ oil. Wheat germ oil is a superb natural Vitamin E supplement, supplying 150·5 milligrams.

Cold-pressed oils

The most beneficial vegetable or plant oils are those produced by the cold-pressed method. The oils of seeds, nuts, grains, beans, olives, and so on are squeezed out by a hydraulic press without heat. The nutrient content of the oils is retained. Other methods, such as screw-pressing or solvent extraction involve great heat which destroys nutrients and unsaturated fatty acids, or the use of chemical solvents which stay in the oils sold to the public.

Sunflower, sesame, and olive oils are most likely to be truly cold-pressed.

Margarines

Making and eating butter dates from ancient times, but margarine was not known until 1860, when it was produced by a French chemist's assistant, Hippolyte Mège Mouriès. His margarine was mainly beef suet. The discovery of the process of hydrogenation early in the twentieth century enabled the hardening of vegetable oils to make margarine, but this produced a saturated fat. Warnings by the American Heart Association and other bodies about saturated fats led to manufacturers inventing soft margarines in the 1960s, labelled 'low cholesterol' and 'high in polyunsaturates'. Though useful; these margarines may still contain saturated fat from a little below sixty per cent to eighty per cent, and artificial colourings and other additives are often used. Those sold in health food stores are the more reliable.

Americans have had more publicity about saturated fats than the British and now eat twice as much polyunsaturated margarine as butter. The British eat twice as much butter as margarine, but the sale of polyunsaturated margarine is now rising.

Carlson Wade, in his *Fact Book on Fats, Oils and Cholesterol*, gives advice on how to de-saturate butter. Soften half pound of butter at room temperature and blend it with one-third cup polyunsaturated plant oil. Add one heaped tablespoon of soy lecithin granules for good measure. When fully blended, refrigerate. To de-saturate milk, mix equal amounts of skim milk and vegetable oil. Blend. The taste and texture is like cream and it can be used like cream.

Using plant oils

You can use the polyunsaturated oils in other ways than de-saturating butter and milk. You can use them for cooking, for tenderising meat, for sauces, and for salad dressings. A simple but good dressing is to mix a plant oil with lemon juice or apple cider vinegar and honey.

With salads you can get the full benefit of the essential fatty acids, lecithin, Vitamin E, and the other nutrients in 'great little seeds'. You can add hulled seeds to the salad and you can toss the greens in a good seed oil, such as safflower or sunflower, or a combination of oils.

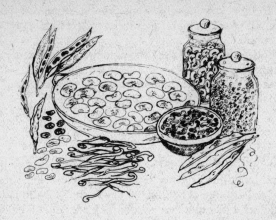

Beans are Beautiful

In this chapter we are considering very important foods for the vegetarian and especially for the vegan, who goes without milk, milk products, and eggs. They are important, also, for any person who cares about the health value of what he eats.

Pulses are among the top vegetables both for flavour and for food value. They provide rich amounts of protein and fibre, the B vitamins, though not B12, phosphorus, potassium, iron, and calcium. Their carbohydrate is also high and so is their energy value. They give excellent amounts of Vitamin A and many give useful amounts of Vitamin C. For fats you will need to look elsewhere, though the amazing soya bean manages to supply even that.

Pulses are well supplied with amino acids, protein's building blocks, and it is only a matter of compensating for some of the weaker amino acids by including at the same meal foods in which they are strong to produce excellent protein. Meat or milk will do it, so, too, will seeds or nuts, grains, or vegetables that have good protein content.

You will get nearly fifty per cent more protein by mixing amino acids in this way.

The impressive nutrient content we have mentioned can be obtained from both fresh and dried pulses.

What are pulses?

The term pulses covers fresh and dried beans, peas and lentils. Pulses are the edible seeds of leguminous or pod-bearing plants. The word pulse suggests life, but comes from the Latin *puls*, meaning pottage. But as pulses are seeds, they are nutritionally 'alive'. When moistened they sprout very easily. You can watch their life unfold, increasing their nutritional value considerably.

Most grocers and supermarkets only offer a limited range of pulses. To delight the eye and to stimulate culinary adventurousness, look for those health food and whole food shops or a continental grocery where there is a dazzling display of beans, lentils and peas, offering variety of size, colour, and shape.

Pulses were one of the earliest cultivated crops, and dried beans, peas and lentils have been found on archaeological sites in South-East Asia that date from about 9750 BC, Egyptian tombs from 2000 BC, Stone Age caves, and Bronze Age dwellings. The ancient Greeks and Romans are thought to have been introduced to pulses by the Aryans, and the Romans took them to Britain. They are now grown throughout the world.

Biblical references to the pulses include Genesis 25:30–4, 2 Samuel 17:28 and 23:11. Daniel 1:11–16 gives powerful support for those people who look upon the pulses as foods for health:

'Then said Daniel to Melzar, whom the prince of the eunuchs had set over Daniel, Hananiah, Mishael and Azariah, "Prove thy servants, I beseech thee, ten days; and let them give us pulse to eat, and water to drink. Then let our countenances be looked upon before thee, and the countenance of the children that eat of the portion of the king's meat: and as thou seest, deal with thy servants." So he consented to them in this matter, and proved them ten days. And at the end of ten days their countenances appeared fairer and fatter in flesh than all the children which did eat the portion of the king's meat. Thus Melzar took away the portion of their meat, and the wine that they should drink; and gave them pulse.'

Adzuki beans

Also known as aduki or azuki beans. Native to Japan. In Japan and China the adzuki crop is second in importance only to the soya bean. Adzuki beans are also grown considerably in South America, the United States, and Zaire. The adzuki bush flowers annually and produces pods containing about twelve small round seeds, mostly dark red, though there are also yellow, brown, and black varieties. The flavour of this pretty bean is sweet and nutty.

Black beans

One of the kidney beans. Large, black, and glossy. Grown in India, China, Africa, and the United States. They are much used in Caribbean cookery.

Black-eyed beans

A variety of cow pea. Small, pale, rough-skinned, and kidney-shaped, with a black mark around its sprouting part that resembles a black eye. It swells a little during cooking, making the skin smooth. Native to Africa, where it is a staple food in many parts. It is now grown in most tropical countries, in the United States, and in Southern Europe.

Borlotti beans

Also known as rose cocoa, crab-eye, or salugia beans. Another bean that is kidney-shaped, with a pinkish speckled appearance. The world's main exporters are Italy, Spain, East Africa, and Taiwan.

Broad beans

Also known as fava beans, haba beans or horse beans. Large and brown. They were eaten by the ancient Egyptians, Greeks, and

Romans, and are now a staple food of poor South Americans. In Brazil, broad beans are roasted and made into flour. Their texture is floury.

Butter beans

Also known as lima beans, sieva beans, curry beans, and pole beans. They were grown on the American continent long before its discovery by Europeans. The early settlers in New England found that the Indian dish *succotash*, made with lima beans and corn, kept out the winter cold. The Indians used to grow the corn and the beans together on the same piece of land. This combination of cereal and bean in one dish balances the strengths and weaknesses of their proteins. The large creamy-white butter beans are popular with the British, who boil them and usually serve them plain, as a vegetable, with meat and potatoes. They can be enjoyed cold with salads. They have a bold savoury flavour.

Chick peas

Also known as garbanzo beans, and in India as gram. These small, round, light-brown seeds have more than 20 per cent protein and rich amounts of Vitamins B1 and B2. They are also rich in magnesium. World annual production is six million tonnes. They are grown in India, Burma, Africa, the Middle East, southern Europe, Australia, and South America. They grow best in hot, dry climates. In some countries chick peas are ground to make flour. Chick peas are used to make *hummus*, a spread, dip or 'starter' that is popular in the Middle East.

Hummus

4 oz (125 g) chick peas
1–2 cloves garlic
2 tablespoons/30 ml
   lemon juice
1–2 tablespoons tahini
   (optional)

4 tablespoons/60 ml
   olive oil
pinch sea salt
pepper

Soak and cook the chick peas until soft. Drain, keeping the cooking water. Mash, sieve, or liquidise the chick peas. Mix with the other

ingredients, adding 4 or 5 tablespoons of the cooking water until
you have a paste with the consistency of thick cream. Season with
salt and pepper.

Cow pea

Cultivated in parts of Africa at least 4000 years ago. Nigeria
produces three-quarters of the world output of one million tonnes.
There are many varieties, the best known being the black-eyed
bean. They have a soft texture and a creamy flavour and are
enjoyable to eat served plain, either hot or cold in salads.

Flageolet beans

Long, slim, and a delicate green hue. Grown in France, Italy, South
America, and Taiwan. The French gave them their name, considering they had a flute-like appearance. They are haricot beans taken
from the pod when young and tender. They can be used like split
peas to make a purée. The French consider flageolet beans excellent
partners for lamb and mutton.

Ful Medames beans

Brown, thick-skinned, pea-sized. Daily fare in some parts of the
Middle East, where they are eaten with the ingredients (described
above) used with chick peas to make *hummus*.

Green beans

These include runner beans, French beans, snap beans, dwarf
beans, stringless beans, and Blue Lake beans, which are purple but
turn bright green on cooking. The Spanish *conquistadors* discovered
them in Central and South America and brought them back to
Europe in the sixteenth century. The Vitamin C content of the
green beans tends to be higher than that of most beans.

Haricot beans

Also known as navy beans (coined by Commodore Perry). Known
to millions of people as the tiny, white, oval beans canned as baked
beans, in which their delicate flavour is almost completely masked

by the flavour of tomato sauce. They are grown either on small bushes or climbing plants. The world's main producers are the USA, Canada, East Africa, Ethiopia, and the Sudan. Cook them yourself and sample their delicate flavour. They are good for casseroles and purées, and can substitute for soya beans in many recipes.

Kidney beans

These beans are kidney-shaped and often have attractive colours. Red kidney beans have a savoury flavour and are much used in Caribbean, South American, and Indian cookery. Pinto ('speckled') and black beans are other members of this family.

Lentils

One of the oldest cultivated legumes, with world production now one million tonnes per year. The seeds are small, only about half the size of a pea. The orange or Egyptian lentil is the most widely available. They are grown in many parts of the world: North Africa, Asia, the Middle East, France, the Netherlands, Germany, and Mediterranean countries. They are also grown in the USA, to which they were first introduced in 1914. They have one of the highest protein contents among pulses, about 20 per cent. They cook quickly and it is not necessary to soak them first. Cooked lentils have a strong, almost peppery flavour. They can be used for soups, stews, and casseroles, and to make rissoles and patties.

Mung beans

Also known as moong beans, green gram, black gram, golden gram, and Oregon pea. Tiny, round, and their moss-green colour does not alter after cooking. They are the most popular bean for sprouting. They can be cooked without soaking. They are native to India, where they are known as *mung dhal*. They are also grown extensively in China, Africa, Thailand, Australia, and the USA. Use in savoury dishes, stews, and casseroles.

Peas

Another food introduced to Europe in the sixteenth century, first to Italy, then to France and Britain. Charles II developed a craving for them, as did Louis XIV who nearly killed himself with excessive eating of peas. Peas were the first vegetable to be canned and the first to be frozen. With freezing most of the Vitamin C can be retained, but with canning most of it is lost.

Soya beans

Also known as soybeans, preta beans, and haba soya beans. Native to China, but also widely grown in Japan, eastern Asia, India, Africa, Australia, South America, and the USA. World production is more than 80 million tonnes.

The soya bean is Queen Bean to the nutritionist. It contains more protein – with all essential amino acids – than any other pulse or vegetable. It is being used to redress protein shortage in some developing countries. It is the only bean with any significant amount of fat.

One cup (180 grams) of cooked soya beans contains:

calories	234	Vitamin B2	·16 milligrams
protein	19·8 grams	(riboflavin)	
carbohydrate	19·4 grams	nicotinic acid	1·1 milligrams
fat	10·3 grams	(niacin)	
fibre	3 grams	phosphorus	322 milligrams
Vitamin A	50 i.u.	potassium	972 milligrams
Vitamin B1	·38 milligrams	calcium	131 milligrams
(thiamine)		iron	4·9 milligrams

One cup (152 grams) of soya bean granules contains 76 grams of protein, and the fermented soya bean paste called *miso* has 47·6 per cent protein.

Two main types of soya bean are grown: the vegetable bean for cooking and eating and field bean for making flour, meal, oil, and other products.

Soya flour can be added to soups, gravies, casseroles, and to flour being used to bake bread. *Soya grits* are tiny pieces of soya beans. Soya beans are hard and breaking up each bean facilitates speedier cooking. *Soya milk* is an alternative for people allergic to cows' milk, and for vegans. It is available bottled, canned, or as a dried powder. It is lower in calcium and Vitamin A than cows' milk, but contains more iron. *Soya oil* is rich in essential fatty acids and lecithin. It is a useful cooking oil and is used in making soft margarines high in polyunsaturated fats. *Tofu* is soya bean curd, pale and smooth, with many uses in preparing meals. Slabs of it can be bought in health food and other stores, such as those supplying a Chinese community.

There are several fermented soya bean products. *Soy sauce* is made by mixing cooked soya beans and roasted wheat and fermenting the mixture by introducing a bacilli called *aspergillus oryzae* and salt. The fermenting time is at least six months but may be extended up to five years. *Miso* is a fermented soya bean cream with a high protein content that can be used in cooking in similar ways to yeast extracts. *Tempeh* is a cheese made from fermented soya beans. Its odour and flavour are both strong.

Texturised Vegetable Protein (*TVP*) is made from soya beans and is a meat substitute that in some uses is difficult to distinguish in taste and appearance from meat.

The wide range of soya products should not be used as a substitute for enjoying the actual cooked soya beans, whose nutritive value and pleasant flavour make worth-while their long cooking time of three to four hours (one hour pressure cooking).

Tic beans

Also known as English field beans, brown Dutch beans, and daffa beans. These are small, round, brown beans which are grown successfully in Britain. Cooked, they have a savoury flavour.

Cooking pulses

Before cooking, dried beans and peas require soaking overnight or for 4–8 hours. (This is not strictly necessary with lentils, but some people soak them also.) They need to be covered well with cold water, at least treble their volume, as most pulses expand to twice their size during soaking. Thorough soaking cuts cooking times considerably and also makes the pulses more digestible. Digestibility is said to be further improved by rinsing them under cold running water following the soaking.

If you do not have time to give pulses a long soak, then pour boiling water over them and leave to soak for an hour, or cover them well with cold water, bring to the boil, simmer for 2–3 minutes, turn off heat and leave to soak for 45–60 minutes.

With adequate soaking, most people do not experience any problems of flatulence. If despite all you do, certain beans produce 'wind', there are other beans you will be able to eat without this problem.

Some cookery experts recommend using fresh water for cooking the pulses, while others say to use the water they were soaked in. Either way, cover the pulses with plenty of water for saucepan cooking. Don't add salt, which toughens pulses and interferes with their cooking, nor bicarbonate of soda which destroys flavour and leaches vitamins. Salt can be added just before serving or at table.

Cook on top of the stove or in an oven already being used. Cooking times vary according to the age and quality of the batch of pulses you have bought. The times given in cookery books can vary widely for this reason. Cook until tender, whatever time it takes. Only a little water should remain when the pulses are tender. The following times given approximate guidance.

Adzuki beans: 25–40 minutes
Black beans: 1 hour
Black-eyed beans: 25–40 minutes
Borlotti beans: 1 hour
Broad beans: 1½ hours
Butter beans: 1½ hours
Chick peas: 1–1½ hours
Ful Medames beans: 1 hour
Haricot beans: 1–1½ hours

Kidney beans: 1 hour
Orange lentils:
    soaked 15–20 minutes
    unsoaked 20–30 minutes
Mung beans: 25–40 minutes
Peas, dried: 25–40 minutes
Soya beans: 3–4 hours
Tic beans: (Field) 30 minutes

Pressure cooking

About a third of the times given above are necessary if you pressure cook at 15 lb per cubic inch. Some pulses froth and may clog the valve of the pressure cooker. This can be avoided by adding two tablespoons of oil to the cooking water. Similarly, a tablespoon of oil for each cup of pulses will prevent any frothing up during saucepan cooking.

Sprouting

Sprouting pulses is a simple process that adds to their nutritional value and produces a food that can be eaten raw and easily digested. Bean sprouts contain active enzymes and the starch in the beans is converted to a simple sugar, which is why they are easily digested. Sprouts carry rich amounts of Vitamins B, C, and E, and supply good vegetable protein.

Soak the beans overnight in a dark place. In the morning, rinse and dry the beans. (I say beans, but you might also be sprouting seeds or cereal grains.) From now on you keep the beans in a wide-mouthed jar or shallow tray covered with muslin, cheesecloth, a stretched stocking, or any other material allowing draining. The beans should be kept moist by rinsing them two to four times daily with lukewarm water. Shake the jar or tray gently as you rinse. Special sprouting trays are sold in health food stores, but a glass jar may be used or any shallow tray.

Harvesting length can be anything from half an inch to two inches long for the larger beans. Some people wait until little green leaves appear, other people prefer to eat the sprouts before then. Average lengths: chick peas $\frac{1}{2}$ in–$\frac{3}{4}$ inch, mung beans 2 inches, lentils 1 inch, soya beans 2 inches. These lengths should be obtained in 3–4 days.

When the sprouts are ready, give a final rinse and remove any shucks (in a colander) and put the sprouts, in a sealed jar, in the refrigerator. They will retain their vegetative vitality for up to four or five days. Eat them raw in a salad or a wholewheat bread sandwich. They can be stir-fried in vegetable oil for some dishes. Mung beans have always been a favourite for sprouting, but all legumes, seeds, and cereal grains give opportunities for sprouting.

Nutrients in one cupful:

	Weight g	Calories	Carbo-hydrate g	Protein g	B1 mg	B2 mg	Niacin mg
Adzuk beans	100	326	58·4	21·5	·5	·1	2·5
Black-eyed beans	165	178	29·9	13·4	·5	·18	2·3
Chick peas	200	720	122·0	41·0	·62	·3	4·0
Green beans, snap, raw	110	35	7·8	2·1	·09	·12	·6
Lentils, cooked	200	212	38·6	15·6	·14	·12	1·2
Red kidney beans, cooked	185	218	39·6	14·4	·2	·11	1·3

Vegetables for Vitality

The title of this chapter is not merely succumbing to easy alliteration. The origin of the word vegetable is the Latin *vegetabilis*, meaning 'animating' or 'full of life'. There is ancient wisdom here, validated by modern science, for the nutrients prominent in most vegetables are those vitamins and mineral salts contributing to bright-eyed, clear-skinned, animated health. It is true that most vegetables have a very high percentage of water – but 'such water!' one might exclaim. If you eat them raw or cook them lightly and in such a way as to retain most of their nutrients, then vegetables will indeed live up to that Latin root from which their English name derives.

The primary dictionary definition of a vegetable is a plant, but in common colloquial use the word has narrower reference to the produce of the vegetable garden or market stall. Thus we sometimes come across the erroneous idea that vegetarians eat nothing but lettuce, beans, and so on. But when the word 'vegetarian' was coined in 1842 it was the Latin word '*vegetus*' that was in mind, meaning 'whole, fresh, lively'. But as other kinds of plant food, beans and peas, are discussed in other chapters, I shall be looking here at those vegetables, mainly greens, bulbs, tubers, and roots, which do indeed fit the popular concept. Most are foods you can grow easily yourself to enjoy maximal quality and freshness. Those you do not grow should be obtained from the best possible source. You may know somebody who has a large vegetable garden or an allotment and who will sell you fresh produce. Or you can buy direct from a farm, or have a reliable market stallholder or local greengrocer. Some health food shops sell organically grown vegetables.

Nutrients in vegetables

Beans, peas and lentils are the best vegetable sources of protein and were discussed in Chapter 10. Soya beans are particularly rich in protein. Most other vegetables are low in protein, especially those that are green and leafy.

The fat content of vegetables is of little significance.

The carbohydrate content varies, being highest in the starchy tubers and roots. Carbohydrate is low in the leafy vegetables. However, all vegetables contain the carbohydrate cellulose which supplies dietary fibre or roughage.

So far, apart from the pulses discussed elsewhere, the nutrient content of vegetables is nothing to enthuse about. The position changes when we come to vitamins and minerals, as a glance at food composition tables show. Running our eyes down the columns for vitamins we notice frequent substantial figures for Vitamin A. There are low figures for the vitamins of the B complex (pulses apart), with a repeated 0 for B12, the vitamin that vegans may miss out on. There are valuable amounts of Vitamin C, especially from the greens. Some vegetables supply Vitamin E. There is no Vitamin D. Vegetables should be fresh and carefully cooked to retain their vitamins. Though the mineral content of vegetables varies according to the nature of the soil in which they grow, most vegetables supply an impressive range of minerals and trace elements. The composition tables show useful amounts of calcium, iron, sodium, phosphorus, potassium, magnesium, iodine, copper, manganese, fluorine, cobalt, selenium, and zinc.

Vegetables are rich in alkaline minerals and should play an important part in maintaining the body's acid-alkaline balance.

It is mainly then for their vitamins, minerals, and fibre that the vegetables discussed here play an essential part in the total diet. Many nutritionists and doctors have pointed out that an increase in certain diseases and disorders has coincided with a decrease in the consumption of fresh vegetables and fruits, with a loss of vital vitamins, minerals, and fibre that is not replaced by refined and chemicalised foods.

A convenient classification of vegetables is according to the part of the plant that is eaten.

Leaves

Dr Richard Willstätter, a German chemist, stated in 1913: 'All life energy comes from the sun, and green plants alone possess the secret of how to capture this solar energy.' Generally the greener the leaf the more nutrients it has, and the outer leaves are richer in vitamins and minerals than the inner leaves.

The greenness in leaves is supplied by the pigment chlorophyll. The outer leaves of a cabbage may have as much as fifty times more carotene than the leaves of its heart. (Carotene is converted into Vitamin A in the body.)

The leaves group is dominated by the cabbage family, which sound more important and exotic if you call them brassicas. Members of the family include cabbage, cauliflower, broccoli, Brussels sprouts and spinach.

The *cabbage* has a commonplace reputation. Millions of people grow them; all you need is a patch of earth. When the walrus in *Alice in Wonderland* said it was 'time to speak of cabbages – and kings', Lewis Carroll was being comic by contrasting the high and the low, the regal and the ordinary. Boiled to a soggy mess, cabbage is a dismal food; warmed up even worse – 'warmed up cabbage wears out the poor master's life', wrote Juvenal. Fresh cabbage, skilfully cooked, can be enjoyable and has lots of goodness. There is a down-to-earth honesty about the cabbage, in its growth, its appearance, and its nutriment. Rabelais saw this and wrote in

Panurge: 'Few and signally blest are those whom Jupiter has destined to be cabbage-planters, for they've always one foot on the ground, and the other not far from it.'

The characteristic smell that comes from the leaves of the brassicas is due to their sulphur content. They also have a high concentration of Vitamin C, which is why we insist that our children eat their cabbage. They also provide useful amounts of Vitamin K and Vitamin A, through their carotene, which is concentrated in the dark green outer leaves. This presents a problem. The outer leaves are the coarsest and most likely to be discarded. These are also most likely to be carrying pesticide residues, as well. You must solve the problem as best you can, using as much of the outer leaves as possible and washing them thoroughly, though quickly, as Vitamin C is water soluble.

Although cooking destroys some vitamins, it does have the effect of making more Vitamin A available from carotene. On average, only about a third of the carotene is converted.

Green and yellow vegetables and fruits are rich in carotene. A cup of steamed *dandelion leaves* supplies more than 27,000 international units (i.u.) of Vitamin A and a cup of steamed kale 8000 i.u. A cup of steamed turnip greens supplies 13,770 i.u. Vitamin A and 81 mg Vitamin C.

Kale is useful in winter when greenstuffs are scarce. It is rich in Vitamins A and C. The fresh leaves are dark blue-green in colour, but otherwise resemble the leaves of spinach. Hard frost actually improves kale's eating qualities.

The *couve tronchuda* or Portugal cabbage can also be tastier when touched with frost. Its large white fleshy ribs can be cooked as *seakale*.

The *collard* is another member of the cabbage family. A cup (150 grams) of steamed collard supplies 11,700 i.u. of Vitamin A and 75 milligrams of Vitamin C.

There are some B vitamins in 'greens' and some protein, and there is a valuable contribution of minerals and trace elements, particularly of calcium and iron.

Brussels sprouts are particularly rich in iron, potassium, magnesium, manganese and zinc.

Spinach is a useful source of carotene, but its nutrient figures are misleading in some important respects. Its oxalic and phytic acids prevent the plant's calcium and iron becoming available to the body. This knowledge was obtained after the creation of the cartoon figure Popeye, who becomes mightily strong after eating a can of spinach.

Chinese cabbage has the least sulphur of the brassicas and its raw flavour is enjoyed by more people because of it. It is very good raw in salads, or cooked lightly.

Most of the brassicas need shredding before they can be eaten raw, which causes some loss of Vitamin C through oxidation, though the loss is not so great as in cooking. Three-quarters of the Vitamin C in cabbage is lost in boiling. Again because of oxidation, chop greens immediately before cooking. B vitamins are also lost in cooking.

Putting bicarbonate of soda in the cooking water helps greens retain their colour, but it also leaches all their Vitamin C. Eat greens immediately after cooking them; don't leave them standing.

If I stuck strictly to classification by what parts of a vegetable one eats, then *broccoli* and *cauliflower* would be classed as flowers. Yes, that firm white curd that is the most edible part of the cauliflower is its flower. Mark Twain described a cauliflower as 'a cabbage with a college education'. We eat the broccoli flower head also. Both cauliflower and broccoli have a good nutrient tally.

Lettuce is the most popular salad plant. The loose leaf type has more nutrients than the crisp varieties.

Raw green leaves make the simplest salad or provide the right start for building a salad. Toss the leaves in a good oil for essential fatty acids and lecithin. You can serve a green salad as a separate course or have it with meat, poultry, fish, rice and other dishes.

Stalks and shoots

If you want to keep down the calories in your diet, you can eat contentedly the stalks and shoots. 100 grams can usually muster only about 15 calories and the water content is about ninety-three per cent. The rest is probably about three per cent carbohydrate, 2·25 per cent protein, and one per cent fibre. Then there are the vitamins and minerals – nothing spectacular in quantity, but useful. The flavour, especially for salads, is always welcome.

Celery was administered as a medicine in the Middle Ages, but at that time it tasted bitter and had a foul smell. We have Italian gardeners to thank for the delightful salad vegetable that celery now is. They blanched the stalks by covering them with earth as they grew.

Celeriac grows as a turnip-shaped root, but the stalks can be cooked and eaten.

Asparagus. The spring shoots or spears are considered rightly a food delicacy. It is best cooked gently and served simply with butter. National preferences in food are interesting, but often puzzling. In Europe the young shoots or spears are cut at soil level and so are white. The British and the Americans prefer green-tipped asparagus, achieved by allowing the spears to grow a few inches above the ground before being cut.

The *globe artichoke* was introduced into England in the seventeenth century, but has never become popular. Henry VIII ate it believing it might ease his painful legs. It is sometimes called Poor Man's Asparagus.

Globe artichokes are grown mainly in Mediterranean Europe and in California. What is eaten is the flower head and fleshy base of the plant. The plant can also be used to produce young growths called chards.

There are just as many surprises in the botany of vegetables as we came across in nuts. Asparagus is a lily, globe artichokes and cardoons are thistles. The *cardoon*, or *Cynara cardunculus*, is allied to the artichoke and has a slightly nutty flavour.

The bulbous base of the stem of the aromatic *Florence fennel* is often used as a medicine. It is good for salads, though it can be cooked as well. The ancient Greeks believed that eating fennel gave them courage and long life.

Chicory is a blue-flowered plant cultivated for its salad leaves and its blanched root. The leaves and stem may be used as raw salad or for cooking as a kitchen vegetable. The root is roasted and ground for use as a coffee substitute.

The taste of *rhubarb* is distinctly sharp, due to its oxalic acid. To sweeten, use molasses sugar or honey. A strange thing about rhubarb – although a vegetable, we eat it as a fruit. But then, we eat the fruits of many plants as vegetables. The Poles, it seems, have a sense of rightness in these matters: they eat rhubarb as a vegetable, mixed with cooked potato.

Roots

Prehistoric man probably scraped up wild roots from the earth to provide winter food. Modern man still finds roots enjoyable, especially when they are young and tender, and carrots, parsnips, beetroots, turnips and swedes are widely cultivated.

Most root vegetables are high in starch, about eight per cent, though with about eighty-nine per cent water they are not too fattening. Protein is usually about 1·5 per cent and fibre one per cent. The range of minerals is excellent, and so is the supply of Vitamin C. There are also useful amounts of Vitamins B1 and B2.

Carrots deserve top billing for their rich content of carotene and so of Vitamin A. A cup (110 grams) of raw carrot will provide 13,000 i.u. of Vitamin A, 7 milligrams of Vitamin C, and 43 milligrams of calcium.

Raw carrot is enjoyable to eat. The greatest concentration of carotene is in the skin and just beneath it, so try to leave the skin intact as far as possible.

The *parsnip*, a member of the carrot family that has been cultivated since Roman times, is much enjoyed for its sweet flavour. A cup (155 grams) of steamed parsnips contains 22 grams of carbohydrate and 19 milligrams of Vitamin C.

The yellow-fleshed *swedes* and *rubages* have more Vitamin A than *turnips*, but turnip greens have high amounts of Vitamins A and C.

Radishes are eaten raw and may be round or elongated. The pink radish can be cooked and its leaves may be eaten. Use raw radishes whole or sliced in a mixed salad.

Salsify, sometimes called oyster plant, has a delicate oyster-like flavour. It and the black *scorzonera* were once popular in Britain and deserve to be better known now. *Celeriac* is a turnip-shaped root that tastes like celery.

Kohlrabi ('cabbage turnip') is worth noting. A cup of raw sliced kohlrabi (140 grams) contains 85 milligrams of Vitamin C, a higher amount than in a similar weight of oranges or lemons.

If you come across them, try some of the less common roots. If you like the taste of aniseed, try *chervil*.

Roots are at their sweetest and tenderest when young and small, except for celeriac which improves with size.

Tubers

One tuber is supreme: the *potato*. It is as plebian as the cabbage, and even more valuable nutritionally.

It is not so fattening as many people think. 100 grams of steamed or boiled potatoes produce 80 calories of energy. The same weight of bread produces 243 calories of energy. Sugar has about five times the calories of potatoes and butter about ten times. Frying potatoes will increase the calorie content threefold, because of the absorption of frying oil.

The English name comes from the Spanish *patata*. The Spanish conquistadors discovered them in Central and South America and brought the tubers back to Europe in the second half of the sixteenth century. At first, the very religious Irish ignored the potato because it wasn't mentioned in the Bible, but by the eighteenth century it had become the staple food there, so that potato blight in the following century caused huge loss of life from starvation and forced emigration to America.

'The potato is a unique food in that it contains virtually all the nutrients required for health,' writes Margaret Knight, a lecturer and examiner on nutrition, in *Teaching Nutrition and Food Science*. No food has all the nutrients in rich amounts. Potatoes contain only a trace of fat, but they do have protein, carbohydrate, fibre, Vitamins A, B, and C, calcium, phosphorus, potassium, sodium, copper, and zinc.

The amount of Vitamin C in potatoes is 30 mg in 100 grams when the tubers are first taken from the earth. Loss of the vitamin increases the more hours pass before cooking and eating. Even allowing for some loss, three medium-sized potatoes can supply minimum daily requirements of Vitamin C. Boiling potatoes in water dissolves up to half the content of Vitamin C.

Drinking milk with potatoes supplements the tuber's protein. A scientist, M. S. Rose, ate nothing but potatoes and milk for four years and stayed healthy.

Baking potatoes in their 'jackets' gives the best return in nutrients, especially if you eat the skins. Boiling them unpeeled is the next most nutrient-conserving method. The protein is concentrated just beneath the skin.

The supermarket practice of selling potatoes in plastic bags causes an early deterioration due to humidity. Exposure to light causes green patches to appear on the skin. These should be cut off as they can be toxic.

Sweet potatoes are long and rounded. They were brought to Britain by Sir Francis Drake, but the British prefer the floury 'ordinary' potato. Louis XV and, later, the Empress Josephine enjoyed eating sweet potatoes. They are well liked today by the Spanish and by the people of some southern parts of the US. Sir Francis Drake said they were more delicious than the sweetest apple. The sweet taste, like that of the apple, comes from their natural sugars.

Another sweet-tasting tuber with natural sugars is the *Jerusalem artichoke*, a knobbly tuber with crisp white flesh. Botanically, the plant is a species of sunflower, *Helianthus tuberosus*. It has become more widely available in Britain since the influx of West Indian immigrants.

Yams look like sweet potatoes (though larger) and taste like them, but they are not related. The skin is wrinkled and the colour varies. The main producers are West Africa, China and Southern Asia. They have a high starch content. Use as you would ordinary potato.

Bulbs

This is primarily the *onion* and family.

The English eat about a quarter of a million tons of onions a year. The French, of course, know their onions, especially when it comes to their culinary uses. They can be cooked in a variety of ways, put in soups, sauces, stews, and savoury dishes, or pickled.

Those grown in cool climates tend to be sharp flavoured, while those grown in hot climates tend to be sweet tasting. Red onions have the most powerful flavour.

The reputation of onions as an aphrodisiac in Middle Eastern and some European countries is hardly justified by their modest nutrient figures. Perhaps the strong stimulating flavour has something to do with it, but there is also the medicinal reputation of onions and its more pungent cousin garlic to be considered. This reputation goes back thousands of years and points to important substances in these two herbs beyond the familiar nutrients.

Onions were used medicinally by the physicians of ancient India, Greece, Rome, and other countries. They have been used for many centuries to ward off infection and were so used, with reported success, during the Great Plague, 1665. Recent analysis shows that the oils of onion and garlic contain phytonicides which kill bacteria. Soviet doctors use the vapour of onions to heal wounds and sores. They pack onion pulp into tubes and hold an open end against the wound or sore for two to ten minutes. Research at the Royal Infirmary, Newcastle gives grounds for believing that onions can help prevent blood clotting.

The French drink onion soup with garlic at the first signs of a cold or 'flu, and modern medical research says much that is in accordance with the French tradition.

While onions are cooked as a vegetable and are themselves components of a meal, *garlic* is too powerful for use other than as flavouring. This it does very effectively.

Garlic, like the onion, is a herb. Its healing powers have been praised by famous herbalists and by the physicians of ancient Egypt, Babylon, Greece and Rome, to say nothing of those of India and the East. Hippocrates recommended it for infectious diseases, Pliny the Elder for respiratory diseases and tuberculosis, and Galen for combatting poisons. Muhammad praised it and Arab physicians have used it for many centuries. Both Daniel Defoe and Samuel Pepys wrote of a family that escaped infection during the Great Plague, whose home became known as 'God's Provident House'. The family had large amounts of garlic in their kitchen and cellar.

During World War II Soviet doctors peeled and cut cloves of garlic and placed them around the edges of wounds. They called garlic 'the Russian penicillin'. Also in Russia, doctors are using a garlic paste to treat pre-cancerous conditions of the lip and mouth. Dr F. G. Piotrowski, of the University of Geneva, gave garlic capsules to one hundred patients with high blood pressure; pressure dropped an average of two centimetres within a week. At a Dublin hospital, garlic inhalants and compresses are used for patients with tuberculosis.

Capsules of liquid garlic are sold in health food shops.

Leeks are another member of the onion family that must be mentioned, for this hardy winter vegetable with the distinctive flavour has superior nutrient figures to onions. In calories, protein, calcium, iron, and other minerals, leeks have a higher content than onions, more than double in most cases.

Shallots are smaller than onions and have a milder flavour. Ovid recommended shallots as an aphrodisiac. They are said to have been brought to Europe by the Crusaders. Martial, the Roman poet, wrote: 'If envious age relax the nuptial knot,/Thy food be *scallions* and thy feast shallot.' *Spring onions* is another name for scallions.

The mild onion flavour of *chives* has been appreciated for more than five thousand years. They bring a distinctive yet subtle touch to salads. They can be grown easily in a garden, window box, or pot.

Vegetable fruits

This group of vegetables averages about ninety-five per cent water, has little protein, no fat worth talking about, and not much carbohydrate; but they contribute useful amounts of carotene, Vitamin C and some minerals, and their flavour is often refreshing.

Aubergines or *eggplants* are large, glossy, and purple, with a slightly bitter taste. They are low in calories, but soak up the fat you fry them in like a sponge. Better to stuff and bake them, or slice them and use for moussaka or ratatouille.

Tomatoes may be eaten raw or used in cooking. They provide useful amounts of carotene and Vitamin C. They are native to Central and South America, but are now widely grown. They were first grown in Europe, in Italy, in the mid-sixteenth century. They can be grown in a sheltered sunny spot outdoors or in a greenhouse or window box. Eat them freshly picked to enjoy their full flavour.

Marrows are more than ninety-seven per cent water, with little energy value, but contribute some calcium, iron, and Vitamin C. They are not palatable raw so need to be cooked. Baby marrows or *courgettes* have a pleasant taste when fried lightly; they can also be boiled or steamed.

Pumpkins and *squashes* are members of the marrow family. The pumpkin is the larger of the two. A native of India, it somehow established itself on the American continent in prehistoric times. It is now grown in many countries.

Hindu physicians in ancient times said that pumpkin seeds were a cure for enlarged prostate gland. The seeds were traditionally used for the same purpose in Russia and other parts of Eastern Europe. Some modern medical research supports the old remedy. The nutritive value of pumpkin seeds was described in Chapter 10.

Sweet peppers are the richest in nutrients of the vegetable fruits.

They can be eaten raw or cooked. The immature peppers are green but when ripe become bright red. The photographer, Edward Weston, with his classic photographs of peppers in close-up, showed the beauty and the eroticism of their contours. Their content of Vitamin C is impressive also, six times that of tomatoes. For nutritional value, eat them raw with a salad.

Sweet peppers belong to the *Capsicum anum* family. Some varieties are ground to make paprika. Chillies are fierce little red or green peppers that will pep up any vegetable dish or may be ground to make Cayenne pepper.

Fungi

The *mushroom* is a fungus which grows as well in darkness as in light. If you go hunting for field mushrooms, make sure that one member of the party can identify the edible varieties. Raw mushrooms have more than ninety per cent water, but they give a fair measure of protein and iron. The non-poisonous wild and the cultivated mushrooms can be eaten raw or cooked. Both kinds supply useful amounts of nicotinic acid, phosphorus and potassium.

Truffles are rather mysterious fungus that grows underground all year. The French made a cult of the truffle in the late nineteenth century. By 1890, the French were consuming two million kilos. Brillat-Savarin called them 'the diamond of the kitchen', and Colette stated: 'If I can't have too many truffles, I'll do without truffles.'

Growing vegetables

Food reformists believe that the quality of the soil in which vegetables grow is improved by organic farming for reasons explained in Chapter 1. A striking example of the influence of soil on crops is the deficiency of iodine in vegetables grown far inland. Some health food stores sell fresh vegetables grown organically without the use of chemical pesticides. Having a vegetable garden or even a vegetable patch is good for domestic economy and provides a source of really fresh vegetables rich in vitamins and minerals and yielding full flavour. Herbs can be grown in window boxes.

Remember to cook vegetables lightly and with minimum use of water so as to conserve their nutrients. Some vegetables can be steamed, but not most roots or tubers. Minimum exposure to air after cutting vegetables is also important.

Including some raw vegetables and vegetable juices in your diet will ensure a good supply of vegetable nutrients.

Nutrients in some vegetables per 100 grams edible portion.

	Calories	Protein g	Calcium mg	Iron mg	Vitamin C mg
Beetroot, boiled	44	1·8	30	·70	5
Brussels sprouts, boiled	16	2·4	27·1	·63	35
Broccoli, boiled	14	3·1	160	1·52	40
Cabbage, raw	28	1·5	65	1·00	60
Cabbage, boiled	8	1·0	52	·60	20
Carrots, young, boiled	21	·9	28·8	·43	4
Cucumber	9	·6	22·8	·30	8
Leeks, boiled	25	1·8	60·5	2·0	15
Lettuce	11	1·1	25·9	·73	15
Mushrooms, raw	7	1·8	2·9	1·03	3
Onions, boiled	13	·6	24·4	·25	6
Parsnips, boiled	56	1·3	35·5	·45	10
Peppers, raw, green, sweet	25	1·00	11	·40	120
Potatoes, baked	100	2·00	13	·70	15 (average)
Potatoes, boiled	80	1·4	4·3	·48	15 (average)
Tomatoes	14	·9	13·3	·43	20
Watercress	15	2·9	222	1·62	60

Fresh and Dried Fruits

Fresh and dried fruits are foods for health that should be part of every person's daily diet. They contain natural sugars, carbohydrates, cellulose (fibre), Vitamins A, B complex, C, and in some cases E. They also furnish iron, calcium, phosphorus, potassium, magnesium, manganese and other trace elements. Most fruits are sweet and refreshing to eat and their juices to drink. Fresh fruits contain eighty to ninety per cent water. If left unsweetened, their calorie content is low but their natural goodness high.

Fruits are particularly good sources of Vitamins A and C.

Vitamin A

The richest source of this vitamin are the yellow fruits. This colour, as with vegetables, signals the presence of carotene, some of which is converted into Vitamin A in the body. Extremely rich in supplying Vitamin A are apricots, cantaloupe, nectarines, peaches, papaya, persimmons, and watermelon. Dried apricots, peaches, and prunes provide powerfully concentrated sources of this vitamin.

Sensible amounts of this vitamin only should be consumed, as it is possible, over a period of time to overdose and damage the liver.

Vitamin C

The crews of the navigators who opened up the world suffered from scurvy, a disease we now know to be due to a deficiency of Vitamin C. The symptoms include extreme fatigue, swollen and bleeding gums, and livid spots on the skin. The famous Captain Cook had this problem with his seamen in the eighteenth century. He observed that there was no sign of this disease among the natives of the islands of the South Pacific, and that lemons were prominent in the diet of these islanders. He gave his crews a daily ration of lemons and had not further problems with scurvy. Any other citrus fruits – such as oranges, grapefruits, or limes – would have been equally effective. The American slang 'limey' meaning English derives from the practice of giving eighteenth-century sailors limes to eat to prevent this disease.

Though the citrus fruits are a good source of Vitamin C, other fruits are even better. Berries are near the top of the table among fruits for Vitamin C. Cranberries from the bogs of Cape Cod, Massachusetts, kept the early whaling crews free from scurvy. Strawberries are particularly rich in Vitamin C, 88 milligrams in a cup (150 grams).

Blackcurrants are justly famed for this vitamin, supplying 200 milligrams in 100 grams of the fruit. A medium-sized guava contains 242 milligrams. But right at the top of the ratings are acerola cherries and rose hips. 10 acerola cherries (100 grams) furnishes 1066 milligrams and a cup of the juice a megadose of 2400 to 5300 milligrams.

Toxic doses of this vitamin are not possible, as the body excretes what it cannot use.

Fibre

Fruits are a good source of fibre because of their high content of cellulose. This is indigestible but is no longer thought inessential because it provides bulk for food passing through the alimentary tract.

Especially high in fibre are apples, apricots, avocado, black-berries (5·9 grams in a cup of them), blueberries, boysenberries, cranberries, blackcurrants, dates, figs, gooseberries, guavas, mango, oranges, dried peach, persimmon, prickly pear, prunes, quinces and raspberries (4 grams in a cup weighing 123 grams).

Dried fruits

Dried fruits merit special mention. They offer the nutritional goodness of fresh fruits in a highly concentrated form. Some fruits are dried by the sun and others by artificial heat. Dried grapes, according to variety, become raisins, currants, or sultanas. The best raisins are made from dried Muscat grapes. Sultanas are made from white seedless grapes. Currants are made from the tiny, purple Corinth grape.

Most dried fruits have a high content of iron. Currants, raisins, sultanas, dried peaches, and prunes, which are dried plums, are particularly good sources. Prunes have natural laxative properties. They should be soaked for at least six hours before use.

Dried apricots contain more protein than any other dried fruit, and its kernel, when crushed, supplies laetrile, sometimes called Vitamin B17, which some researchers claim can check the growth of cancerous tumours. California, Australia, Iran and Turkey are the world's leading suppliers of dried apricots.

Dates and figs are among the world's oldest cultivated fruits. The date palm produces prolifically and trees live up to a hundred years and more.

Health food stores provide packets of mixed dried fruits that are superb for snacks and for use with *muesli* and all breakfast cereals. They can also be used with salads, desserts and other dishes. Whatever dish they are added to, they will furnish rich concentrations of potassium, iron, phosphorus, sodium, magnesium, sulphur, and silicon.

Exotic fruits

While making full use of the familiar fruits, you should miss no opportunities to try less familiar varieties. Many now popular fruits were once considered exotic. There are exciting flavours to be discovered and in terms of a healthy diet you cannot go wrong. These fruits should be eaten fresh if possible, but some of them you may wish to cook. Shops catering for the tastes of ethnic minorities often provide unfamiliar fruits and vegetables and are worth a visit. The owners are usually very helpful in giving information about their produce. If fresh fruit is not available, then canned fruit will have to do.

If I mention some names, it will turn out that some fruits are familiar to some readers. Americans tend to be more familiar with tropical and subtropical fruits than British people. But here goes.

Breadfruit (the indirect cause of the mutiny on HMS Bounty), Bullock's Heart, Cape gooseberry, carambola, citron, durian, guava, jakfruit, kiwi fruit (Chinese gooseberry), kumquat, langsat, litchis, mango, papaya, passion fruit, prickly pear (fruit of cactus), rambutan, rozelle, soursop, ugli (but nice; cross between grapefruit and tangerine).

The *papaya* is worthy of further mention. It is the fruit of a tropical American tree. Half a medium-sized raw papaya supplies 2625 i.u. of Vitamin A, and a cup of the canned juice a massive 5000 i.u. of Vitamin A and 111 milligrams of Vitamin C. Hernando Cortez discovered the papaya in Yucatan and planted it on Mexico's western coast. There it was discovered by Captain Cook who took it across the Pacific. In some primitive societies there is the belief that the plant is half human because it produces male and female flowers on separate plants. The leaves contain papain, an enzyme that tenderises meat.

Fresh is best

Fresh fruit provides the highest concentration of vitamins and minerals, and the most delectable flavours. Freezing fruit soon after picking is next best. Canning causes loss of nutrients.

Fruit should be washed in case pesticide residues are on the skin. You may wish to skin them if particularly worried about this, but by doing so you lose the vitamins in and just under the skin. Some fruits have to be peeled anyway. Skin thinly if you do skin an apple, pear, or other fruit.

Wild-fruits (e.g. blackberries) should not be picked at roadsides because of contamination from the lead in car exhaust fumes. The effects of lead poisoning were described in Chapter 1.

Fruit juices made from fresh fruit are real health drinks, rich in Vitamin C.

	Weight	Calories	Carbo-hydrates	Vit. A	Vit. C	Iron	Potassium
	g		g	i.u.	mg	mg	mg
Acerola cherries							
raw 10 fruits	100	23	5·6		1066	·2	68
juice 1 cup	242	56	11·6		3872	1·2	
Apple, raw 1 med.	180	96	24·0	150	7	·5	182
Apricot, raw 3 av.	114	55	13·7	2890	11	·5	301
dried 1 cup	130	338	86·5	14,170	16	7·2	1273
Banana, raw 1 av.	150	127	33·3	270	15	1·0	550
Blackberries 1 cup	144	84	18·6	290	31	1·2	245
Cantaloupe, raw	100	30	7·5	3400	33	·4	251
Currants, black	100	54	13·1	230	200	1·1	372
Dates 10 med.	100	274	72·9	50	0	3·0	648
Guava, raw 1 med.	100	62	15·0	280	242	·9	289
Lemon 1 med.	110	20	6·0	10	39		102
Mango, raw 1 fruit	300	152	38·8	11,090	81	·9	437
Orange 1 av.	180	64	16·0	260	66	·5	263
Papaya ½ med.	150	58	15·0	2625	84	·45	351
Prunes, dried							
1 cup	185	411	108·0	2580	5	6·3	1117
Strawberries 1 cup	150	56	12·6	90	88	1·5	246

Health Foods from the Sea

The 'Mother of Life'

Scientists tell us that life began in the sea. Some of the sea species eventually crawled on to land and learned to survive there. Some scientists say that we are descended from a kind of jellyfish while others propose a new theory of evolution tracing our history back to seaweed. Dr Lawrence S. Dillon, Professor of Biology at Texas A. & M. College, studied changes and developments in the internal structure of living cells and announced:

'All animals are in reality a type of high, modified, plant life, derived a billion years or so ago from a common ancestry with the brown seaweed. We are forced to conclude that all life belong to only one kingdom, which in all honesty must be recognized as the kingdom of plants.'

Whatever the true story of the evolution of life, we should look to the fact that our blood is saline and chemically similar to sea water. Consider two remarkable facts: the sea contains all the mineral salts the human body needs for its well-being; and secondly the composition of seven gallons of sea water and that of the human body is almost identical.

The major constituents of sea water are boron, bromine, calcium, carbon, chlorine, fluorine, hydrogen, magnesium, oxygen, potassium, sodium, strontium and sulphur. These make up 99·997 per cent of the total dissolved salts and are found everywhere in virtually the same proportions. There are over eighty minor mineral constituents, including actinium, chromium, cobalt, copper, iodine, iron, phosphorus, radium, silicon, uranium and zinc. It also contains small amounts of gold.

Fritz Haber, a German chemist, organised a sea expedition with the aim of paying off the total German war debt with gold extracted from the sea. The gold is there all right – about one-hundred million dollars' worth in a cubic mile of sea. The trouble is that the cost of extraction would be greater than the value of the gold.

Fully practical, however, is the idea of recovering some of the sea's vast mineral riches through consuming fish, kelp, carrageen moss, agar-agar, and other sea foods – nutritional gold, one might say.

Land and sea

Constantly the sea becomes richer by denuding the land of its mineral salts. Erosion and leaching are forms of such pirating and rivers dissolve soluble minerals from the soil and carry this rich booty to the sea. Rachel L. Carson wrote in *The Sea Around Us*:

'The ocean is the earth's greatest storehouse of minerals. In a single cubic mile of sea water there are, on the average, 166 million tons of dissolved salts, and in all the ocean waters of the earth there are about 50 quadrillion tons. And it is in the nature of things for this quantity to be gradually increasing over the millenia, for though the earth is constantly shifting its component materials from place to place, the heaviest mutations are forever seaward.'

Farming is another factor in depleting the earth of its mineral wealth. Valuable trace elements are missing from the soil of certain regions in most countries, which means a corresponding lack in vegetables grown there. The US Department of Agriculture has published pamphlets discussing the problems caused by a deficiency of cobalt in the soil in parts of New England, the middle Atlantic States, Florida, Wisconsin and Michigan. Cobalt is necessary for the manufacture of Vitamin B12 in the body and its lack is related to anaemia and some other disorders. Other areas of the USA have soils deficient in copper, selenium, and other trace elements.

Dr H. Curtis Wood wrote in *Overfed and Undernourished* (paperback *Calories, Vitamins and Common Sense*), Exposition Press:

'Our earth-grown vegetables can only contain the elements that are made available to them in the soil in which they are grown. Therefore it is progressively more unlikely that we can obtain the trace elements that we need even from a diet that is well-balanced and contains plenty of fresh vegetables.

'The ocean, on the other hand, is the greatest storehouse of minerals and, while the exact composition of its waters may differ a bit in various areas, the mineral content is relatively constant as compared to the soils of the world ... It is in the nature of things for this quantity to be gradually increasing, as the rivers of the earth carry precious top soil ever seaward. Every hour of every day the land is getting poorer and the ocean richer, as far as these vital minerals are concerned. Therefore, because of the wealth of minerals in the sea, ocean-grown plants have all these substances available to them and are found to contain a greater number of these elements in greater quantity than the land-grown species.'

Some authorities see the sea as the best potential source of food supply for a rapidly increasing world population. At least nine countries are manufacturing fish flour for human consumption; every part of the fish goes into it, finely ground. Off-putting, if you start picturing it – but highly nutritious, and one answer to the world shortage of protein. The flour is processed in a way that takes out the fishy taste and may be used, like wheat flour, for baking bread, cake, macaroni, and so on.

If the food potential of the sea is not to be marred by industrial pollution, governments will need to work together to combat this growing problem. Mercury poisoning of Japanese coastal dwellers has highlighted the danger.

Sea foods

Fish, shell-fish, and edible seaweeds make the minerals of the oceans available for human consumption. Dr D. C. Jarvis, in his best-selling *Folk Medicine*, writes:

> 'In the sea there is and can be no deficiency. Every element necessary for life is present everywhere, and the living animals and plants of the ocean select what they require. Sea foods are capable of supplying all the elements necessary in our foods, whether we know what they are or not. In sea foods the necessary elements not only have been selected and assimilated on the basis of the natural requirements of living tissues, but they are stored and available in the form of a natural food in something approaching the proper proportions of the diet of man.'

Fish

Fish not only supply such essential mineral salts as calcium, iodine, iron, phosphorus and potassium, but also Vitamins A and D and protein in a more easily digested form than animal meat. Vitamins A and D are concentrated particularly in the fish liver oils, especially those of fat fish. Fat fish include bloaters, herrings, kipper, salmon, sardines, sprats and whitebait. Lean or white fish include cod, haddock, plaice, sole and turbot. Bream, hake, halibut, mackerel, trout and sturgeon could be described as 'in betweens'. The fat fish are higher in calories than lean fish, a fact worth noting by slimmers.

Even though there is a wastage of fifty per cent or more on fish bought whole, fish meat is one of the most concentrated and economical sources of protein. In terms of edible portion, the protein content of tuna, sardine, salmon, kipper, herring, haddock and other white fish is a little higher than that of beef, mutton or pork.

Fish meat in most cases is more easily digested than animal meats. It is easily absorbed in the intestines. The structural looseness of fish meat compared with the density of animal meat can be observed in handling. Lean fish are more easily digested than fat fish.

Fish lends itself to a wide variety of cooking methods, but one should avoid overcooking – simmer rather than boil, for example. Remember that in some countries raw fish is considered to be a great delicacy.

A last point in favour of fish: fish fat is unsaturated and so is not harmful to the heart and arteries, as the saturated fat in animal meats can be. With saturated fats, fish could not survive in cold water, for hard fats solidify at low temperatures. Fish developed an especially soft fat that is actually *more* unsaturated than vegetable oils.

Edible seaweeds

Health food stores and mail order suppliers of health foods provide the nutritional riches of the sea through the edible seaweeds such as kelp, carrageen moss and agar-agar.

It is noteworthy that farm animals that browse by the shore usually display robust and handsome health. Sheep and cattle, given the opportunity, will feed on driftweed. When dried seaweed is included in the diet for cows it improves milk production. Hens that feed by the seashore or have dried kelp added to their diet lay eggs that have hard shells and firm yolks. The quality of Orkney and Shetland wools is not unconnected with the number of sheep which feed on the shores of those islands.

Seaweed grows in the rich 'soil' of sea water and is loaded with the sea's mineral salts. 'Sea herb' or 'sea spinach' would be a more deserving description than 'weed'.

It is gathered, dried, and eaten along the shores of many countries. The Japanese are especially partial to it. The Welsh wash and boil laver (*porphyra*), a thin red seaweed, then mince it until they have a kind of green porridge called 'laver bread'. It may be eaten with bread and butter or served up for breakfast with strips of bacon. A preparation made from this kind of seaweed was used in ancient China to cure dropsy.

Kelp

Dry or boiled seawood is not to everybody's taste. Fortunately, it can be bought pressed in tablets, as powder, or in dried sticks. A heaped teaspoonful of kelp powder will make a pint of jelly that sets rapidly. As it is tasteless, it is advisable to add fruit juice or other flavouring. It can be used in stews, stuffing, casseroles, and sauces.

There are about 900 known specimens of kelp, a large olive-brown algae, but most kelp tablets are processed from *fucus vesiculosus*, because plenty of it is available. As a child, you may have 'popped' with the soles of your feet air bubbles on its flat fronds. The Japanese lead both in the farming of kelp and in its consumption. Its stem is called a 'hold fast'. The plant is attached to a rock in the sea and matures after two years; after one year it grows even when taken from a rock. Rotation farming is thus possible.

Kelp supplies a cornucopia of mineral salts supporting human health.

Composition of kelp

Calcium	Copper	Sugar (fucose)
Potassium	Tin	Carbohydrate (starch)
Sodium	Lead	Fats
Aluminium	Vanadium	Protein
Iodine	Zinc	Vitamins A, B, D, and E
Iron	Barium	
Magnesium	Chromium	
Strontium	Titanium	
Manganese	Silver	
Silicon		

The sugar (fucose) does not raise the sugar level of the blood and so is not harmful to diabetics.

With such a rich mineral content, it is hardly surprising that kelp has a reputation as a healer. Its mineral salts and vitamins help normalise the main body processes: metabolism, blood pressure, the heart, arteries, glands, liver, pancreas, gall bladder and kidneys all benefit. Iodine is essential for normal functioning of the thyroid gland. Goitre is an enlargement of the thyroid gland caused by lack of iodine. Magnesium helps to keep bones, teeth, and nails strong. Manganese helps keep the nervous system healthy. Copper has a part to play in the formation of haemoglobin and helps the body to utilise Vitamin C. There is more calcium in the human body than any other mineral element: it is part of bones and teeth and its presence in the bloodstream and soft fluids is essential for muscle tone and blood clotting.

Dr D. C. Jarvis, author of *Folk Medicine*, mentions five patients whose arthritis improved after taking one kelp tablet each morning for a year. Dr J. W. Turrentine, of the US Department of Agriculture, said: 'Of the fourteen elements essential to the proper metabolic functions of the human body, thirteen are known to be in kelp . . . It should be made available for all people in all lands.' The recommended daily dosage of kelp is one five-grain tablet a day. Take an extra one if you feel you have a special therapeutic need.

Carrageen moss

Carrageen or Irish moss (*chondrus crispus*) takes its name from a place on the west coast of Ireland. Narrow *chondrus* is used as food, the wider variety is put to industrial use. An Irish moss industry operates on Ireland's Atlantic seaboard, in the maritime provinces of Canada, around Scituate, Massachusetts, and in Brittany, where it is known as 'lichen carrageen' or 'gloemon blanc'. The plant is gathered, washed, dried, and bleached, making the moss hard and wiry to the touch. Soaking it provides an extract which may be used in preparing foods. Its commercial uses depend on its powers to stick, gell, suspend, emulsify, and stabilise. It is used in making ice cream, chocolate milk drinks, salad dressings, sauces, toothpastes, emulsions, lotions, shampoos, cosmetics, and so on.

Carrageen moss, like kelp, contains a near perfect balance of the mineral salts essential to our health. Its natural properties are retained in the product sold in health food and some other stores. Its mineral salts include bromine, calcium, iodine, magnesium, potassium, and sulphur. The gelling element is gelatinous ethereal sulphate. The moss itself is not consumed: an extract is prepared by soaking it. Its most obvious use is in drinks and jellies. Add fruit juice or other flavouring. It is also of value in the preparation of soups, salads, bread, pies, pastry, blancmange, trifle, soufflé, sauce, and other foods.

Recipes

Note that 1 oz (25 g) of carrageen equals one ordinary sized breakfast cup packed tightly.

Carrageen milk drink

pinch of carrageen   sugar and flavouring
1 pint (500 ml) milk

Wash the moss and leave to steep for 10–15 minutes. Pick out any
black or discoloured parts. Put into a saucepan with the milk, pinch
of salt and lemon rind (or other flavouring). Bring slowly to the
boil until the carrageen coats the back of a wooden spoon. Add
sugar and stir until dissolved. Strain and serve in a warm glass.

Carrageen soufflé

1 pint (500 ml) milk   ¼ pint (125 ml) cream
½ oz (14 g) carrageen   1 tablespoon sherry
1 oz (25 g) sugar)   chopped pistachio nuts
1 egg (separated)   whipped and sweetened cream

Prepare a soufflé mould by tying a band of doubled paper around
the outside of the mould. The paper should come about 2 inches
(5 cm) above the top of the mould. Steep the carrageen for 10–15
minutes. Pick off any discoloured parts. Put it with the milk into
a saucepan and cook until it coats the back of the spoon. Beat the
yolk of the egg with the sugar and flavouring and strain the
carrageen on to it. Whisk well until it begins to set. Fold in half
the whipped cream and the stiffly beaten white of egg. Pour into
the prepared soufflé mould or into individual glasses. Leave until
set and carefully remove the paper. Decorate with roses of cream
and sprinkle pistachio nuts over.

Carrageen blancmange

¼ oz (7 g) carrageen   3 cups milk
¼ teaspoon salt   3 teaspoons sugar

Steep carrageen for 10 minutes in water, drain, add to milk with
salt, boil slowly for 15 minutes (or 30 minutes in double saucepan).
Add sugar to taste (flavouring if desired with lemon peel, malt,
syrup, vanilla or almond essence), strain into mould, serve when
cold.

Irish fruit jelly

$\frac{1}{4}$ lb (100 g) redcurrants
$\frac{1}{4}$ lb (100 g) blackcurrants
$\frac{1}{4}$ lb (100 g) raspberries
2 bananas, sliced

1 oz (25 g) carrageen
1 cup granulated sugar
1$\frac{1}{2}$ tablespoons lime juice

Soak the carrageen for 10 minutes and drain off water. Simmer in 1 pint (500 ml) of water for 15 minutes. Press the currants through a wire sieve and add to the juice the sugar, lime juice, raspberries and sliced bananas. Pour into the saucepan containing the carrageen and bring to the boil. Strain the mixture into goblets and place to cool and set. Serve with whipped cream.

Carrageen trifle

3 small sponge cakes
jam
$\frac{1}{4}$ pint (125 ml) cream
sherry or fruit juice
$\frac{1}{2}$ oz (14 g) carrageen

1 pint (500 ml) milk
pistachio nuts (chopped)
angelica
cherries

Cut the sponge cake and spread liberally with jam. Place in open dish, pour on sherry or fruit juice and allow to soak. Prepare carrageen. Simmer for 20 minutes in 1 pint (500 ml) milk. Strain, sweeten to taste and pour over. Garnish with chopped nuts, angelica cut into diamonds, etc., and cherries.

Carrageen cream cheese

1 pint (500 ml) sour milk
$\frac{1}{4}$ cup (7 g) carrageen

pinch of salt

Soak carrageen in cold water for 10 minutes. Strain and pick over. Boil rapidly for 15 minutes in $\frac{1}{2}$ pint (250 ml) of water. When carrageen is almost cool, place in a muslin bag with the sour milk and hang up to drain off whey. Empty contents of bag into a basin, add pinch of salt and beat together with fork for a few minutes. When set cut in squares.

Carrageen milk beverage

Soak $\frac{1}{4}$ oz (7 g) carrageen in water for 10 minutes. Drain. Add to 1 pint (500 ml) of milk and simmer for 10 minutes. Strain and sweeten to taste and serve hot.

Agar-agar

Agar-agar has the rapid gelling powers of carrageen moss. It is sometimes called Oriental or Japanese isinglass or Japanese gelatin. It is produced from kinds of red algae that attach to rocks. Divers gather it in Japan and in California. It is bleached, boiled, frozen, thawed, and dried, and sold as powder, flakes, shreds, or bricks. It is widely used in the food manufacturing industry in much the same way as carrageen moss. It contributes to the pharmaceutical industry and to dentistry. Japan has the largest share of the world market. Its Japanese name, 'kanten', means 'cold sky'.

The public mostly buys agar-agar as a powder, and like carrageen moss it is relatively inexpensive. The jelly made from it is mildly laxative. Fruit juice or other flavouring needs to be added. Its therapeutic possibilities – like those of the edible seaweeds in general – await exploration, but one interesting property of agar-agar is worth mentioning: scientists have found that it carries small negative electrical charges.

Sea salt

Most health food stores can supply sea salt crystals which have been evaporated under natural conditions. They can be used in cooking or to sprinkle on food at table, after grinding them through a wooden mill. The flavour is subtle and attractive.

However, a word of warning is necessary. Do not let what has been said above about the great mineral wealth of the sea mislead you into thinking that liberal use of salt in cooking and on food at table will be health-enhancing. Sea salt is superior nutritionally to the more widely used salt, but there are grounds for the view that salt in general should be used sparingly.

Salt is mainly composed of sodium and chloride, and an excess of sodium can be harmful to health. Many foods in the average

Western diet naturally contain quantities of sodium. Unless you work hard in hot weather or in hot conditions which cause excessive sweating, you are unlikely to go short of salt.

Maurice Hanssen, in *About the Salt of Life* (Thorsons), says that 'not using salt in cooking and doing without at table' is 'a good general dietetic suggestion for those who consider themselves well.' And a low-salt diet is a *must* for people suffering from high blood pressure, hardened arteries, or Ménière's disease. Experiments have shown that a low intake of sodium reduces the risk of a build up of cholesterol deposits in the arteries. Other studies reveal that the harmful effects of an excess of sodium can be offset by a compensating higher intake of potassium.

It is worth noting that herbs make a delightful and varied substitute for salt in cooking.

Supplements: Gambles and Certainties

Are supplements necessary?

Who needs dietary supplements? The simple answer is any person whose diet is deficient overall or in some departments.

But there are two further questions that have to be asked. The first question is, how does one know which nutrients are lacking or whether the diet as a whole is deficient? Obviously, low levels of vitality and poor health would be one possible answer. Other people will have a more problematic neutral body awareness, and for them a more scientific approach is necessary. Study food composition tables, work out how much of each nutrient you are getting, and see how the totals match the daily allowances recommended by government health bodies.

Now we are approaching that other question. The prime essential is to raise the overall level of nutrition with a sound basic diet based on the foods discussed in this book, whole natural foods that provide their full nutritional riches. Proteins, fats, carbohydrates, water, fibre, vitamins, minerals and trace elements should be obtained in good amounts and in healthy balance. The question is; having done that, are supplements necessary even then?

A supplement, a dictionary says, is 'an addition to anything, especially one making it more perfect or complete'. The illogicality here does bring out well the point under discussion. Something that is perfect or complete cannot be made more so. Some doctors make the point that buying health foods, and supplements in particular is a waste of money, because most people have a diet already adequate in nutrients. Including supplements, by this argument, would be like trying to put wine in a bottle already full.

This criticism is heard less often now than a few years ago. More and more eminent physicians are pointing to the connection between poor standards of diet and the degenerative diseases. And health foodists surely have justification in turning the criticism round and exclaiming, 'what a colossal waste of money the way millions of people buy devitalised and adulterated foods denuded of both nutrients and natural flavour!'

But the question still remains for the reader who is concerned about the quality of what he eats and who is trying to make his or her diet complete. Are supplements still necessary? Ideally, they shouldn't be. But the main consensus of opinion among food reformists is that supplements have a part to play for most people, either by filling a deficiency in one or more nutrients or by raising nutritional standards overall. Maximal health and sense of well-being are goals for most people, with diet probably the most important consideration.

An athlete training for the Olympic Games, with already a high level of physical fitness, will continually aim for even greater strength, speed and endurance, and probably take dietary supplements. Likewise, non-athletes are not eccentric if they use supplements to fortify their diet or aim to attain excellent health and vitality.

Adelle Davis points out in *Let's Get Well* that farmers feed many supplements to their livestock on top of a diet already designed for their good health. She discovered that American farmers were using thirty-two supplements for dairy cows, twenty-nine for race horses, twenty-four for laying hens, twenty-two for steers, and twenty-one for hogs, to say nothing of those for sheep, goats, and other animals. These supplements furnish concentrated proteins, essential fatty acids, and many minerals and vitamins, including several frequently omitted from human supplements. Farmers give their livestock a diet designed for excellent health and add supplements of concentrated proteins, minerals, vitamins and other nutrients. Should we treat ourselves less favourably?

You can feel well and still reasonably want to feel even better. There is nothing cranky or hypochondriacal about this aim.

A final point in favour of using supplements. Calorie needs are lower today than they used to be when work and getting about was physically harder. Many people have a problem to keep their weight at a healthy level. So the question arises for these people, and not only these people, of making their calories count. Here supplements have a part to play, for they provide a rich concentration of nutrients; their calories are 'full', not 'empty'.

It seems to me that supplements do have something to offer of value to most people with food values what they are today. At any rate, the certainties among the supplements have something to offer most people. I use the terms certainties and gambles to distinguish between those supplements whose content of nutrients and whose effects are largely known. For example, bran provides fibre which is often lacking in the modern diet, and wheat germ has such a concentration of B vitamins, Vitamin E, and other nutrients that there can be no doubts about its potential value.

In the gamble class I place ginseng and the beehive products pollen, propolis and royal jelly. Analysis of their properties is incomplete and much mystery and doubt surround their supplementary values. The gambles may or may not work wonders for you. There is no evidence that they will do you any harm, which cannot be said of many popular foods on which much money is spent today. There are likely to be readers whose experience of those supplements I am calling gambles is so positive that for them my gambles are their certainties.

I will concentrate in this chapter on what I consider to be the main certainties and a few of the most interesting and potentially rewarding gambles, leaving aside the many elixirs, potions, powders, pills and capsules that belong to the treatment of specific diseases and disorders. Sound natural nutrition will build up resistance to disease, and disease can be treated by diet. But essentially good nutrition is concerned with health and that has been the approach of this book.

Desiccated liver

This is beef liver that has been dried in a vacuum at a low temperature so that there is little loss of the original nutrients. In some forms the fat and cholesterol have been removed. It is available as tablets and as powder. It should not be cooked, but used as it is in soups or with any food in which you find it palatable.

The dried liver contains a powerful concentration of protein, Vitamin A, the whole Vitamin B family, Vitamin C, Vitamin D, Vitamin E, iron, calcium, phosphorus, potassium, and other minerals.

A quarter cup (37 grams) of defatted desiccated liver supplies:

calories	120	patothenic acid	5·5 milligrams
protein	28 grams		
Vitamin B1 (thiamine)	0·2 milligrams	Vitamin B12	18·5 micrograms
		Vitamin C	70 milligrams
Vitamin B2 (riboflavin)	4·4 milligrams	iron	6 milligrams
		calcium	10 milligrams
nicotinic acid (niacin)	11·3 milligrams	phosphorus	600 milligrams
		potassium	480 milligrams
cholin	370 milligrams		
inositol	74 milligrams		

Brewer's yeast

Yeast is a tiny fungus plant which can multiply at a phenomenal rate. In contact with sugar it causes fermentation and produces alcohol and carbon dioxide. Brewers are interested in the alcohol and breadmakers in the carbon dioxide which makes dough rise.

Dried brewer's yeast, a by-product of brewing, makes a marvellous dietary supplement. Vegetarians and people not attracted to dried liver can obtain a very rich concentration of protein, nearly 40 per cent, and all the B group vitamins, iron, phosphorus, potassium, and other minerals from brewer's yeast. It has a protein content well above that of meat. It contains sixteen amino acids, including all eight essential amino acids, seventeen vitamins, and fourteen minerals.

Brewer's yeast is used in some mental hospitals, as its B vitamins are believed to benefit some mental disorders. It contains the nucleic acid RNA which is thought by some researchers to delay the effects of old age and the degenerative diseases.

A tablespoon of powder a day should not be exceeded. Large quantities over a long period could cause irritation of the kidneys.

A tablespoon (8 grams) of debittered brewer's yeast supplies:

calories	23	pantothenic	1 milligram
protein	3·1 grams	acid	
Vitamin B1	1·25 milligrams	phosphorus	140 milligrams
(thiamine)		potassium	152 milligrams
Vitamin B2	·34 milligrams	iron	1·4 milligrams
(riboflavin)		calcium	17 milligrams
nicotinic acid	3 milligrams		
(niacin)			

Wheat germ

Yet another rich plant source of protein, the B vitamins, Vitamin E, iron, phosphorus, and potassium. It also contains vegetable oil and essential fatty acids. The oil is sold separately and is extremely rich in Vitamin E, 21·5 milligrams in a tablespoon (14 grams). To get the same amount from other top sources you would need to eat 2½ pounds (1 kg) of fresh herrings or a cup of raw almonds. A cup of wheat germ itself provides 15 milligrams of Vitamin E, and with it you get protein, B vitamins, and many other nutrients not in the extracted oil: 26·6 grams of protein, 9·4 milligrams of iron, all the B vitamins, calcium, phosphorus, potassium, magnesium, copper, selenium, and zinc.

The structure of the wheat berry was explained in Chapter 3. The germ is tiny, only three per cent of the grain, but it contains more than half of the grain's total content of vitamins. The germ and the outer protective bran are discarded in milling white flour.

Both are available from health food shops and some other stores as dietary supplements.

Dr Wilfrid E. Shute, an international authority on Vitamin E, writes in his *The Complete, Updated Vitamin E Book**:

'The Food and Nutrition Board of the National Research Council (NRC) has estimated the adult requirement for alpha tocopherol (Vitamin E) to be between 20 and 30 i.u. per day. Because of changes in the processing of essential and basic foods over the last 70 years, it is very doubtful that many people today receive anything close to 30 i.u. per day ... Typical diets in Great Britain, for example, have been estimated to contain less than 5 i.u. Most commercial vitamin pills contain no Vitamin E. There is none in most of the foods in the average American diet.'

Vitamin E helps protect the blood vessels and the heart from disease, assists the healing of wounds, protects against virus infections, and has properties which have caused it to be dubbed 'the rejuvenation vitamin'.

Vitamin E has been used extensively in treating infertility. Dr Evan Shute, a Canadian, compared 1973 expectant mothers untreated and 825 treated with wheat germ oil. Fifteen per cent of the untreated women aborted compared with only 3·7 per cent of the women taking wheat germ oil with its high content of Vitamin E. Premature births and toxaemia were much reduced in the treated patients.

Because of its oil, wheat germ should be kept covered and refrigerated to prevent rancidity. Most people find its slightly nutty taste attractive. It can be eaten with milk (combining amino acids), sprinkled on *muesli* or other cereal and eaten with milk, cream, or yogurt, in vegetable stuffing, pancake batter, soups, and so on. On ice cream it tastes like chopped nuts. Add a teaspoon of wheat germ to each cup of baking flour.

One cup (100 grams) of raw wheat germ contains:

---

* From *The Complete, Updated Vitamin E Book* by Wilfred E. Shute. Copyright © 1975 by Wilfred E. Shute. Published by Keats Publishing Inc., New Canaan, CT. Used with permission.

calories	363	pantothenic acid	2·2 milligrams
protein	26·6 grams	Vitamin E	15 milligrams
unsaturated fat	8·18 grams	iron	9·4 milligrams
Vitamin B1 (thiamine)	2 milligrams	calcium	72 milligrams
Vitamin B2 (riboflavin)	·68 milligrams	phosphorus	1118 milligrams
		potassium	827 milligrams
		magnesium	336 milligrams
Vitamin B6	·92 milligrams	copper	1·3 milligrams
folic acid	·328 milligrams	selenium	88·3 milligrams
nicotinic acid (niacin)	4·2 milligrams	zinc	14·3 milligrams

Bran

Bran, like wheat germ, is discarded in milling white flour. A cup (57 grams) contains 9 grams of protein, B group vitamins, 4 milligrams of iron, other minerals and trace elements. Its very high content of plant cellulose, 5·2 grams, makes bran the perfect supplement to ensure adequate fibre in the diet. This was discussed in Chapter 5.

Bonemeal

Bonemeal is made by grinding cattle bones into a fine flour. It contains very high amounts of calcium, also phosphorus and the trace elements copper, manganese, nickel, and fluorine, minerals that keep teeth and bones sound and strong. Bonemeal checks dental decay and has special value for the pregnant woman and her unborn child.

Soya products

The unique vegetable protein content of the soya bean was discussed in Chapter 10. A cup (152 grams) of soya bean granules contains a huge 76 grams of protein and a cup (100 grams) of fermented soya beans (miso) 47·6 grams of protein. Soya bean products can be looked upon as useful supplements. One or two teaspoons of soya flour may be added to each cup of flour used for baking.

Fish liver oils

These are extremely potent sources of Vitamin A. One tablespoon of cod-liver oil supplies 11,900 i.u. of Vitamin A and 3·6 milligrams of Vitamin E.

Molasses

This by-product of the processing of white sugar contains the minerals and vitamins of the sugar cane. It is unrivalled as a source of potassium and has more calcium than milk. It can be used as a sugar substitute, though the taste is slightly bitter. It is described in Chapter 2.

Dried skim milk

This has little fat but is high in protein, calcium, Vitamin B2 (riboflavin), and other valuable nutrients. It can be used in making breads, soups, yogurt, sauces, junkets, and so on. Unless you are on a low-fat diet, it can also be stirred into whole milk to fortify it.

Lecithin

Lecithin is naturally present in virtually every cell in our bodies. It prevents the accumulation of fat in the liver and research shows that it helps control cholesterol by acting as an emulsifier, reducing the risk of hardened fat narrowing the arteries, high blood pressure, and heart attacks. In the 1960s in Britain, heart attacks almost doubled in men between the ages of twenty-five and forty-four.

The lecithin sold in health food shops contains more than seven per cent linoleic acid, an essential fatty acid which has a key role in the body's control and absorption of fat.

It is available either in granular or liquid form. Egg yolks are rich in lecithin, but also in cholesterol. The lecithin sold as a supplement comes mostly from soya beans, another rich source. It is sometimes labelled 'soy phosphatides'.

Lecithin has proved successful in treating cases of psoriasis and of eczema in children. Normal supplementation would be 1–2 tablespoons daily.

Kelp

Seaweeds contain the nutrients of the mineral-rich sea which are constantly renewed, as explained in Chapter 13. Kelp is the most familiar of the more than 400 varieties of seaweed. Some readers may know it as bladder wrack. To the ancient Chinese, Greeks and Romans, it was a medicine as well as a food. It also makes a very good fertiliser.

Kelp tablets make an ideal supplement for anyone wanting an impressive range of minerals and trace elements. Eating the seaweed itself is neither practical nor enjoyable for many people, though the Japanese and others consider it a delicacy.

Kelp contains thirteen vitamins, twenty amino acids, and sixty trace elements, according to one analysis. Perhaps its most important contribution as a supplement is its supply of the trace elements, about which science has still much to discover.

Alfalfa

Alfalfa products are available as supplements and have similar uses to those of the soya bean. There is alfalfa cereal, flour, tablets and powders. There is even an alfalfa tea, which is made from the leaves of this leguminous plant whose cultivation is among the earliest.

It has six times the protein of milk and is a rich source of calcium, iron, potassium, chlorine, and magnesium. It contains B group vitamins, including B12, and is among the best sources of Vitamins K and U. (Vitamin K helps normal clotting of the blood and healthy functioning of the liver.)

Rose hips and acerola cherries

Rose hips grow at the base of rose blossoms and are bounteously rich in Vitamin C, as well as being good sources of Vitamin A, the B group, Vitamin E, Vitamin K, and the bioflavonoids (Vitamin P). The bright-hued substances collectively known as bioflavonoids are found in the edible parts of fruits but are not in their juices. They are necessary for the absorption of Vitamin C. By using a natural supplement like rose hips you obtain Vitamin C (ascorbic acid) with its natural support.

Acerola cherries are another excellent source of Vitamin C and they are sometimes combined with rose hips in natural supplements.

Multi-vitamin/mineral supplements

These can be synthetic or natural. Leading natural sources of vitamins and minerals have already been given, but some readers may wish to have the insurance of a multi-vitamin/mineral tablet. This should not be necessary if you are eating a proper diet and obtain the vitamins and minerals from other natural supplements. But ... it is tempting to 'make sure' with one tablet that taken daily gives all the main vitamins and minerals. Usually the makers try to provide minimum daily requirements, but often leave out the important Vitamin E and some other valuable substances. Every precious substance for healthy nutrition cannot be packed into one pill. It is important that a multi-vitamin/mineral tablet should not be considered cause to avoid the necessity of planning a healthy diet.

Synthetic vitamin/mineral supplements contain the identical structure of the natural supplement. Are their effects then identical? Tests have shown the superiority of natural supplements, though the synthetic supplements are not ineffectual, and they often save lives. Synthetic supplements often contain artificial colourings and flavourings and stabilising salts like acetate, bi-tartrate, palmatate, and so on, whereas the natural supplements contain natural supportive co-factors, like the bioflavonoids with the Vitamin C in rose hips and fresh orange juice. Vitamins are still being discovered, as are other valuable substances in foods, and such actual or possible natural support is missing from synthetic 'pure' supplements, however useful they may prove in hospital work.

Recommended daily allowances

There is reason to believe that the following figures of Recommended Dietary Allowances of the National Research Council, published by the National Academy of Sciences in America, 1974, may be looked upon as minimum targets to reach. Many writers on natural nutrition consider that obtaining higher (though not excessively higher) amounts will benefit health and make allowance for the falling nutrient standards of foods.

	Men	Women
carbohydrates, grams	390	300
fats, grams	87	66
protein, grams	56	46
calcium, milligrams	800	800
iodine, micrograms	110	100
iron, milligrams	10	18
magnesium, milligrams	350	300
phosphorus	800	800
potassium average daily intake, milligrams	1950–5850	
Vitamin A, i.u.	5000	4000
Vitamin B1 (thiamine), milligrams	1·2	1·0
Vitamin B2 (riboflavin), milligrams	1·5	1·2
Vitamin B6 (pyridoxine), milligrams	2·0	2·0
Vitamin B12 (cyanocobalamin), micrograms	3·0	3·0
nicotinic acid (niacin), milligrams	16·0	13·0
Vitamin C (ascorbic acid), milligrams	45·0	45·0
Vitamin D, i.u. adequate daily intake	400 i.u.	
Vitamin E, i.u. adequate daily intake	15·0	12·0

Pregnant and lactating women require additional protein, calcium, iodine, iron, magnesium, phosphorus, Vitamins A, B1, B2, B6, B12, nicotinic acid, C, and E.

Gambles from now on – though probably there will be readers for whom they are certainties.

Apple cider vinegar

The remarkable thing about apple cider vinegar as a health food and dietary supplement is that its position was established by one man – Dr D. C. Jarvis – and his best seller *Folk Medicine*. He worked among the tough mountain folk of Vermont, USA for half a century, and supports their medicinal use of apple cider vinegar, mixed with honey, for many human and animal ailments. He also has some things to say on the importance of iodine and kelp.

Dr Jarvis' theory about why apple cider vinegar is a healer is based on the acid reaction it produces in the body. This appears to be the opposite tack to most writers on natural healing who recommend an increase of alkaline-forming foods in the diet. Jill Wordsworth, about the only writer on health foods I have come across whose approach to the subject is neutral, observes with puzzlement in *Diet Revolution Food Reform*:

> 'Here we have books which sold a million copies and founded an industry but the idea behind it all has vanished into oblivion. Only the cider vinegar remains ...'

The health-restoring formula is simple: two teaspoons apple cider vinegar in a glass of warm water sweetened with a little honey. Also use apple cider vinegar for French dressings, etc.

Ginseng

This Oriental herb fascinates the media and the general public alike, because there is something exotic and mysterious about it. Scientists are testing it, and the results are encouraging enough to stimulate further research.

For thousands of years in China and other parts of the East ginseng has been looked upon as a rejuvenator and booster of health. It features in early Chinese treatises on herbal medicine. The plants grow to about two feet tall and bear bright red berries, but it is the thin pale root often resembling the human figure – ginseng means 'man plant' – that is of value. On Korean farms the ginseng crop is protected by men in watch towers on stilts.

Inevitably, where there is a legend a certain amount of mumbo-jumbo and hugger-mugger attend claims to the effects of eating ginseng or drinking tea made from it. This has until recently obscured the real value of the herb, but gradually a picture is emerging of an anti-stress food and general tonic, a booster of the life force rather than a specific curing this or that ailment or disease. This is in keeping with the Oriental approach to healing, which generally is holistic, meaning wholistic.

Though tests produce some positive results, researchers find it difficult to pin-point the constituents of the herb that might justify its reputation.

Professor E. J. Shellard, of the Pharmacology Research Laboratories, Chelsea College, University of London, writes:

> 'Ginseng does not appear to possess any specific well-defined pharmacological action, but rather exhibits a large number of

different pharmacological activities, all of which contribute towards its total therapeutic effects.'

And Professor Wesselin Petkov, of the Faculty of Pharmacy, Institute for Specialised and Advanced Medical Training, Sofia, wrote in 1968:

'The positive effect of ginseng on the reactivity of the organism, particularly on the central nervous system, is the master-key dissipating the mystery of the favourable impact observed on widely divergent conditions unrelated to each other either pathogenetically or etiologically. It is this phenomenon also which throws light on the improvement wrought by ginseng on the mental and physical capabilities of man.'

In the nineteenth century Western physicians investigated ginseng and pronounced that it was of no medicinal value. Today many papers are being read by medical scientists at international conferences and there is now considerable interest in it.

In Japan and Russia ginseng is given to workers in car plants to reduce lost man hours through sickness and to improve efficiency. Sales of ginseng in Western stores are rising.

There is no precise dosage. In work with laboratory animals it has been found that large doses can sometimes reverse the effects. In the East ginseng is recommended for seasonal use in the autumn and winter. That the action of some drugs can be influenced by seasonal rhythms of the body has been shown by Western studies and opened up a branch of study called 'ecological pharmacology'.

Despite ginseng's reputation as an enhancer of virility and sexuality, it is clearly not a stimulant and good results, if they come, will be over a period of weeks and months rather than days.

The Russians have their own 'Siberian ginseng', which is an extract from the shrub *eleutherococcus*, a thorny creeping plant of the same family as ginseng. Tests indicate that it helps animals withstand various stresses and acts as a general tonic, like ginseng. Russian athletes were given it as a supplement in their preparation for the 1980 Olympic Games.

Pollen, propolis, royal jelly

As great an aura of mystery surrounds these three products of the beehive as envelops ginseng.

Pollen is described by the Oxford English Dictionary as: 'The fine granular or powdery substance produced by and discharged from the anther of a flower, constituting the male element destined for the fertilisation of the ovules.'

Bees carry plant pollen in their pollen sacs to their hives and store it as food. Until recently one could obtain lots of pollen in honey, but the practice of filtering now removes much of it. Scrapings from the bottom of the hive are rich in it. Grains of pollen are so minute that more than 14,000 of the largest grains weigh only one gram.

Analysis of the constituents of pollen are far from complete. It contains twenty amino acids, including the eight essential amino acids, according to a Swedish study, and the B family vitamins riboflavin (B2), nicotinic acid (niacin), pyridoxine (B6), pantothenic acid, biotin, inositol, and folic acid. There is also some Vitamin A, C, D, E, and K, and choline and rutin. Eleven enzymes have so far been discovered, and the minerals include calcium, iron, potassium, magnesium, and sodium.

Scientists in Sweden, Yugoslavia, and elsewhere have found that pollen, propolis, and royal jelly may give immunity against colds, influenza, and other infections. Other investigations have been into the use of pollen in treating patients with enlarged or inflamed prostate glands. A combined German–Swedish study with 172 men resulted in relief of prostatis (inflammation) in seventy-six cases.

Propolis is the resin which the bees use for sealing in their hives. Here, analysis has proved even more difficult than in the case of pollen. Propolis contains five per cent pollen, the rest being resins, waxes, balsams, and oils. Like pollen, propolis may protect people against virus infections.

Much research remains to be done into propolis and into the effects of eating *royal jelly*, which is the special food that bees feed to queen bees. It is a glandular secretion of the worker bees. The queen bee grows to nearly twice the size of the worker bees.

In France, Mexico, and some other countries royal jelly is being prescribed for arthritis. The Toltecs of Central Mexico have for centuries looked on it as a rejuvenator, a reputation it also has with some African nomadic tribes.

Royal jelly has been found to contain pantothenic acid, pyridoxine (Vitamin B6), biotin, and nucleic acid, all substances that might well play important roles in delaying ageing. But much analysis and research waits to be done.

Tablets made from these beehive products are available. A month's course or longer could be tried in the autumn with a view to building up resistance to winter infections.

Planned supplementation

You may decide on permanent supplementation of your diet. A good case can be made for bran and wheat germ. Or you may wish to economise and take some of the more expensive supplements for a month or so in late autumn to build up strength for the winter months. Athletes and sportsmen may wish to try them in the weeks coming up to an important contest.

Most supplements are sold with instructions for safe quantities. The following are suggestions for average daily use.

> Brewer's yeast: up to 1 tablespoon
> Wheat germ: 1–2 tablespoons
> Bran: 1–3 tablespoons
> Molasses: 1 tablespoon
> Lecithin: 1–2 tablespoons
> Apple cider vinegar: 2–4 teaspoons

Few of the writers on nutrition who favour vitamin and mineral supplements are willing to state amounts for average use. An exception is Dr Carlton Fredericks who, in *Eating Right For You*, recommends as 'a good investment' daily: Vitamin A 10,000 units; Vitamin D 500 units; Vitamin C 250 mg; Vitamin B1 2 mg; B2 4 mg; B6 4 mg; niacin 50 mg; pantothenic acid 20 mg; B12 10 micrograms; Vitamin E 50 mg for the person who has been eating whole grain for years and 100 mg for up to two years 'for the person who has eaten like the average American'; calcium 250–1000 mg, according to the amount of milk and cheese in the diet; phosphorus 180–750 mg; iron 15–18 mg; magnesium 150–270 mg; manganese 1 mg; iodine 0·15 mg; zinc 20–100 mg.

Large doses of B complex vitamins and Vitamin E have produced improvement in people suffering from mental disease. Large doses – 1500–3000 mg daily for three days – of Vitamin C is believed to prevent a cold caught at the first signs. A deficiency of Vitamins B1 and 2 can produce irritability, fatigue, nervousness, fears and so on, which lift quickly when the deficiency is corrected. Extra Vitamin C is needed at times of stress.

If you are a smoker and can stop the habit, at a stroke you will start absorbing more Vitamin C and B group vitamins. You will also save a lot of money and get more value from your normal diet.

Whatever questions arise for you about the use of dietary supplements, the important thing is to give them a fair test, at least for a month. Then see how you feel. Be quiet, be still, and allow your 'body wisdom' to speak.

Your Health! What to Drink

Water

Water is essential for human survival, but if you want to drink it pure then you will have to put up with its being very boring. Distilled water is pure water, free from bacteria, but few people would make it the only thing they drink for long. Distilled water is not only free from bacteria, it is free from the minerals that give water its taste. Water tastes differently according to its mineral content and the part of the earth from which it comes. Differences in water make a considerable difference to the flavour of beers, stouts, teas, and so on made from it.

Mineral waters come from various natural springs and supply iron, calcium, and various trace minerals.

In some places fluoride is added to drinking water to check the rate of dental decay. Such moves are opposed by some people who question the long-term safety of the addition of this chemical.

Researchers from the University of Turku in Finland found more than double as many bone fractures among 237 elderly people receiving fluoride treatment than among those not taking fluoride. They came to the conclusion that too much fluoride contributes to osteoporosis and broken bones in aged people. This study was reported in the *British Medical Journal*, 12 July 1975.

In the United Kingdom it is found that cardio-vascular disease is higher in areas with soft water supply than in those with hard water supply. Hard water contains more calcium, but there is a theory that the more acidic soft water dissolves elements from the soil that may cause cardio-vascular disease.

We need to drink about 1300 ml of water a day. We get another 850 ml in our food, and the oxidation of protein, fat, and carbohydrate gives us another 350 ml. This total of 2500 ml (about 5 pints) is balanced by a daily loss of the same quantity of water by evaporation from lungs and skin and in urine and faeces.

Few people are prepared to drink nothing but water. They prefer it to be flavoured in some way.

Fruit and vegetable juices

These can be bought bottled in health food stores, but nothing beats making your own using fresh fruits and vegetables. They contain rich amounts of the vitamins, minerals, and trace elements that are in the fruits and vegetables that are squeezed or liquidised. The nature of these nutrients was described in Chapters 11 and 12.

Parsley juice provides rich quantities of Vitamin A and C. Carrot juice is unequalled for Vitamin A, though remember that a few years ago a man in England drank gallons of it over a short period, turned red, and died from cirrhosis of the liver. A dramatic example of the need for moderation even with health foods! A glass or so a day will do nothing but good, and as well as the Vitamin A from the carotene you will also get calcium, iodine, potassium, sodium, and sulphur.

Cabbage juice provides Vitamins A and C, and calcium, iron, and other minerals and trace elements.

One glass (8 oz) of orange juice provides 112 calories of energy, 500 i.u. of Vitamin A, 129 milligrams of Vitamin C, ·5 milligrams of iron, 27 milligrams of calcium, phosphorus, potassium, and other mineral salts.

The vitamins and minerals in fruit and vegetable juices can be augmented by mixing juices to combine strengths. Herbs can provide subtle flavouring and trace elements.

Tea and coffee

Though the use of tea originated in China as a medicinal herb, it is now thought to contribute little nutritionally, apart from some fluorine, the trace mineral that is in bones and teeth. The benefits of drinking tea are mainly psychological – the 'cup that cheers'. People opposed to the use of even mild stimulants criticise tea for its caffeine, which provides the 'lift' it gives. Caffeine is also present in coffee. Tea's tannin is also criticised.

I am discussing now what I might describe as 'ordinary' tea, the tea from India, Sri Lanka, and elsewhere whose drinking the British, at home and abroad, have made an institution. Herbal teas, which in herbalism have medicinal use, are sold in a wide range in health food stores. Yet, interestingly, ordinary or regular tea, as we may so distinguish it, is also a herb and was widely praised for its powers to revive physical energy and the spirits when the Chinese first began drinking it.

Tea-drinking in China, according to Chinese folklore, is attributed to the Emperor Shen-Nung who, in 2737 BC, was boiling water for drinking when leaves of the wild tea tree dropped into the water and gave it an attractive flavour. For hundreds of years the Chinese drank tea for its medicinal properties: it was described as being very good for overcoming 'lethargy of the body'.

The tannin in tea provides its dark colour. High concentrations of tannin, or tannic acid, can harm the lining of the mouth and digestive tract. Cancer of the oesophagus (gullet) is higher among tea drinkers than non-tea drinkers, but the danger is obviated if you drink milk with your tea in the British manner.

Tannin is present in the skins of fruits and in herb teas, though not with such concentration as in ordinary tea.

Caffeine excites the nervous system and the brain, raises blood pressure, and activates the metabolism. In moderate quantities and strengths these effects are mild. If tea or coffee is drunk excessively and is very strong it can cause disturbances of the nervous system, heart, and circulation, such as palpitations and chest pains. It may also cause irritation of the kidneys.

Caffeine, like the nicotine in cigarettes, is an alkaloid to which people can become addicted, so that giving up drinking coffee or tea can produce withdrawal symptoms. Sensitivity to caffeine varies with the individual. It speeds up the heart rate and may cause abnormalities of heart rhythm. The effects on the heart are similar to those produced by nicotine, and smoking and coffee drinking are often a shared addiction. The amount of caffeine in one cup is as follows: Brewed coffee 100–150 mg; instant coffee 60–80 mg; decaffeinated coffee 3–5 mg; tea 40–100 mg; cola drinks 17–55 mg.

Americans have the world's top caffeine intake, mainly from coffee, which is made from the coffee bean, but also from tea, chocolate, cocoa, and cola drinks. A bottle of cola contains about as much caffeine as is in one-third of a cup of coffee of medium strength. American college kids have been known to get 'high' on it, using a technique which I need not describe.

People with heart or nervous disorders should drink tea and coffee moderately, in both quantity and concentration, or cut them out entirely.

People who experience no unfavourable reactions and are keen on their 'cuppa' and have no objections to mild stimulation need be careful only of avoiding excess. Tea and coffee drinking for many people has social, psychological, and ritualistic value. The Japanese have their 'tea ceremony', in which tea is prepared and drunk with friends in poised and calm awareness. Millions of people in the West do the same without self-consciously ritualising it. Relaxation and stimulation are balanced.

Readers not familiar with herbal teas should lose no time in sampling them. Varying what you drink can be to the benefit of health.

Coffee substitutes

Health food shops sell coffee substitutes, which should be tried. Coffee addicts will not find that they taste like the real thing, but will probably find that some can be enjoyed as alternative drinks in themselves.

Postum is made by mixing molasses and bran and roasting them, then adding red wheat and grinding the mixture.

There are Swiss coffee substitutes that include grains, fruits, and roots.

Toasted grains are the basis of several coffee substitutes. The cereals used include wheat, bran, barley, millet, rye, and oats. Chicory is another coffee substitute.

The dried and ground roots of dandelions make another coffee powder.

Decaffeinated coffee powder is also available, though I have read that in removing the caffeine an ingredient gets into the coffee that some people are unhappy about.

Herb teas

Herbs were once in common use in Europe, lost popularity in the eighteenth century, but are now enjoying a revival for both culinary and therapeutic use, if the number of books published on herbs is anything to go by. The book illustrations are often a joy to the eye, as the aromas of the herbs in a herbal shop can be a delight to the nostrils.

Most herbs can be bought already dried from herbalists and the common varieties from health food shops. If you want to go in for picking your own, the best time for picking is a sunny morning in spring or early summer.

Herbs provide essential trace elements often lacking in the modern diet. The curative value of herbs is well attested, though their work is subtle and takes time. There is said to be a herb for every human ill. Thousands of years of experimentation has produced present knowledge of their therapeutic uses. Soon after writing was invented about 5500 years ago, the first records of herbal medication appeared. Most of the herbs were already identified by the Middle Ages.

The value of herbalism is neatly summarised by Mrs C. F. Leyel in *The Truth About Herbs*:

> 'Herbs, or medicines made exclusively from plants, are the natural cure for human disease and ill-health. Plants alone have the power of building up organic life from inorganic material. Unlike the drugs, which are inert, they are made from organic material instead of inorganic substances, and form an active or *living* medicine.'

Herb teas provide refreshing drinks that contain the health-enhancing properties in plants. They are sold as dry leaf or as tea bags. If a newcomer to herb teas, buy several and try them. Much later, you may like to try mixing herbs, such as a strong herb with a mild one. Herbal teas are made as for ordinary tea, that is, by infusion, preferably using a stainless steel or ceramic teapot. Use one teaspoon of dried leaves for each cup of tea. Pour boiling water on the leaves and leave for five to ten minutes, which is longer than you would leave ordinary tea to brew. Pour into a cup and drink it as it is or with a teaspoon of honey or a slice of lemon.

The therapeutic uses of hundreds of herbs can be studied in the many books written on this subject.

As with regular tea, herb teas should not be drunk excessively. Up to four cups a day should be safe, but it should be pointed out that some are diuretics, or have other properties that should not encourage plentiful drinking for pleasure. What dangers there may be in drinking herb teas is brought out by Linda Clark in *How To Improve Your Health*. People who criticise tea and coffee often fail to mention possible dangers from excessive drinking of herbal teas. For normal use, it is important to vary the herb teas and at the same time to drink and vary other liquids.

Dr Ronald K. Selig, of the University of California, found that at least 396 commercially available herbs and spices could produce mind-altering symptoms, and Linda Clark warns that some herb teas may cause kidney irritation, gastro-intestinal disturbances, respiratory problems, convulsions, and other disorders. The disturbances are in fact identical in most cases with those possible from excessive drinking of ordinary tea.

Beer and wine

Here again there are dangers to health in excessive drinking, more obvious and widely-known than those attached to drinking too much tea or coffee. But in moderation, they are not unhealthy, and there are social and psychological benefits from drinking beers and wines. Wine, the product of fermented grapes, is one of the purest drinks there is. It is a daily table drink in grape-growing countries.

There is much pleasure to be had from making your own beers and wines, both in the preparation and in the drinking. Often, however, they can be more powerful than commercial beers and wines.

Spirits, which are produced by distilling rather than fermentation, are stronger in alcohol and provide nothing nutritionally apart from calories. Beers and wine supply carbohydrates, small amounts of protein, B family vitamins, sodium, potassium, calcium, magnesium, and manganese.

Most beers are made from barley, hops, sugar, yeast, and water. Hops have healing properties according to gypsy and some peasant folklore. In Britain a movement for the real old-type ale has been gathering strength fast. Enthusiasts for 'real' ale look on it the way health foodists look on stoneground wholewheat bread compared with white bread.

Alcoholism is such a problem in so many countries that scientists are reluctant to publicise some of their findings. An American Heart Association meeting in Anaheim, California, in 1979, was told that moderate drinking of alcoholic beverages was good for the heart. *Macleans* magazine, 11 February 1980, reported Dr Terence Anderson, professor of epidemiology at the University of Toronto's faculty of medicine, as saying: 'If this was not something with an addictive or hazardous potential, we'd be shouting it from the housetops. If it was Brussels sprouts that did this, who'd be hesitating?' And he added: 'It's embarrassing from a public health point of view, but life is full of these dilemmas where a little bit is good and a lot is bad.'

A little bit is good and a lot is bad. This applies to every beverage I have discussed. And it also applies to every health food I have written about in this book. You can get too much even of a good thing.

Eating for Health: A Summary

Now you have read the preceding chapters of this book, you should have picked up the salient features of eating for health. A summary though may be appreciated.

You will have understood that there is much to be gained from basing your diet on natural whole foods that have not had nutrients taken from them (refining) or anything added to them (chemical additives).

Diet seems the most likely primary link with the 'diseases of civilisation' – the degenerative diseases which have grown to epidemic proportions in the twentieth century in the West. Natural nutrition can build up resistance to disease and offers protection against stress and degenerative diseases.

As far as possible, buy whole foods that have been organically grown and are free from pesticide and other chemical residues.

Acquire knowledge of the basic principles of sound natural nutrition. Read about it in this and other books. Be wary of diets based on a restricted list of foods. Eating a wide variety of wholesome foods is your best plan for obtaining a balanced supply of nutrients.

There are six essential nutrients: proteins, fats, carbohydrates, water, vitamins, mineral salts. To these we might add plant cellulose or fibre.

Proteins, water, and mineral salts work together for repair and growth of tissues; fats, carbohydrates, and proteins provide fuel for body energy; and vitamins and mineral salts act as regulators of body activity.

Proteins can be obtained from animal sources: meat, poultry, eggs, milk, cheese (Chapter 7). Animal food proteins are similar to human proteins in composition. Plant proteins are obtained from whole grains, nuts, seeds, and pulses (Chapters 3, 8, 9, and 10, respectively). Plant proteins should be mixed together at one meal or mixed with animal source proteins for optimum 'completion' of their amino acids (protein's building blocks).

Fats can also be obtained from both animal and plant foods. The former sources include meat fat, fish oils, milk, cream, and butter; the latter sources include seed, nut, grain, olive, and soya bean oils. While there are dangers to health for some people in animal fats, vegetable fats contain polyunsaturated oils and essential fatty acids that protect the heart and arteries from a build-up of hard fat (Chapter 9).

Carbohydrates, which include sugars and starches, are the body's main suppliers of fuel for combustion and energy. Healthful sources of carbohydrate are whole grains (Chapter 3), tubers and roots (Chapter 11), and pulses (Chapter 10). Refined white sugar is almost entirely denuded of the nutrients naturally present in the sugar cane or sugar beet. Alternative sweeteners that do supply nutrients along with energy are described in Chapter 2. Natural sugars are present in fresh and dried fruits, vegetables, milk, and other foods.

Water has a vital role in the functioning of the human body and makes up about seventy per cent of body weight. Vary what you drink so as to obtain any positive benefits from particular beverages and to avoid any dangers to health possible from any single beverage. What to drink is considered in Chapter 15.

Until recent times adequate plant cellulose or fibre in the diet could be taken for granted, but no longer. The importance of dietary fibre is discussed in Chapter 5. Fibre adds bulk to the food passing through the intestinal tract, keeps it moist and moving, and ensures regular effective daily bowel emptying. Cereals, vegetables, and fruits supply fibre, and a tablespoon or two of wheat bran makes the perfect supplement.

Foods for health naturally supply rich amounts of vitamins and mineral salts, both of which have key roles in the body's internal activities. A deficiency of vitamins or minerals leads to disease.

Vitamins may be divided into two groups: the fat soluble Vitamins A, D, E, and K, and the water soluble Vitamins B and C. Vitamins A and D are found in oils and fats and Vitamins B and C mainly in vegetables and fruits. There is some loss of Vitamins B and C in cooking water, so cook lightly and retain cooking water for stock.

Vitamin A was the first vitamin to be discovered, in milk. It is needed for the health of the eyes and a deficiency causes infection of the eyes, night blindness, and blindness itself in some underdeveloped countries. Rich amounts are available from fish and animal fats. Fish liver oils top the table. Other good sources are liver and dairy products. Another major source is through the carotene in green and yellow vegetables. Carrots top the table, and other excellent sources are watercress, apricots, lettuce, and other green vegetables. The carotene is converted into Vitamin A in the body. Fish obtain carotene from the plankton they feed on. Vitamin A stands up well to boiling, but there is some loss in hot frying.

Vitamin D is the anti-rickets vitamin. We need it for the absorption of calcium and phosphorus and the soundness of our bones and teeth. The best food sources are similar to the animal sources of Vitamin A: fish liver oils, fatty fish, bonemeal, eggs, milk, butter, and cheese. Sunlight is another source, as it converts into Vitamin D a chemical substance ergosterol which is stored in the skin.

Vitamin E is linked with fertility and protection against the diseases of old age. The richest sources are wheat germ oil, wheat germ, cold-pressed vegetable oils, whole grains, wholewheat bread, eggs, liver, desiccated liver, nuts, green vegetables, and peas.

Vitamin K is needed for normal blood clotting. Richest sources are dark green vegetables, soya beans, tomatoes, molasses, liver, meat, and egg yolk.

The water soluble *B complex vitamins* include B1 (thiamine), B2 (riboflavin), B3 (pantothenic acid), B6 (pyridoxine), B12 (cyanocobalamin), nicotinic acid (niacin), and folic acid. The quantities of B1, B2, and nicotinic acid for many foods have been listed in the preceding chapters. They are needed for metabolism. B6 may help women who suffer from pre-menstrual tension. B12 is needed for the formation of red blood cells, and is obtained from liver, fish, meat, eggs, milk, and cheese. Richest sources of B1 are brewer's yeast, wheat germ, molasses, liver, meat, whole grains, nuts, and pulses. Best sources of B2 are brewer's yeast, whole grains, molasses, liver, meat, milk, cheese, nuts, and pulses. For nicotinic acid: brewer's yeast, meat, fish, poultry, whole grains, peanuts, milk and milk products.

A deficiency of *Vitamin C* (ascorbic acid) causes scurvy, fatigue, swollen gums, and slow healing of wounds. The richest sources are fresh fruits (Chapter 12) and vegetables (Chapter 11), especially rose hips, acerola cherries, blackcurrants, strawberries, citrus fruits, broccoli, cabbage, green peppers, parsley, and watercress.

Inorganic or *mineral salts* make up about seven per cent of body weight. Those present in the body in minute, but essential, amounts are called trace elements. Main minerals are calcium, phosphorus, iron, potassium, chlorine, sodium, and magnesium. Trace elements include iodine, fluorine, cobalt, copper and zinc.

Raw and lightly-cooked vegetables are excellent sources of mineral salts, as are the seafoods discussed in Chapter 13. Vary the vegetables you eat and try some that are new to you. For the more exotic vegetables and fruits, shop at specialist suppliers to ethnic minorities.

Meats, milk, cheese, nuts, vegetables, and whole grains supply calcium, phosphorus, and potassium. Liver, meat, eggs, whole-wheat bread, and green vegetables furnish iron. Seafoods, eggs, vegetables, and whole grains supply iodine.

Kelp is a cornucopia of mineral salts and available as tablets. Other valuable dietary supplements include brewer's yeast, desic-cated liver, wheat germ, bonemeal, and dried skimmed milk. The case for using some form of supplement is put in Chapter 14.

Cultivate 'body wisdom', awareness of how your body reacts to foods.

Balance and moderation are good rules for all aspects of living, particularly in diet. Whatever the merits of a single food, drink, or dietary supplement, it should have only a balanced place in the total diet, which is what really counts in eating for health.

Remember that part of eating for health is cooking for health. This means cooking vegetables lightly to conserve their vitamins and minerals.

Enjoying the full flavour of whole foods is also important. Eating for health and eating for enjoyment can become one, especially if you cultivate skill in preparing and cooking foods for health. Books on whole food cookery will prove good investments both in terms of encouraging a healthy diet and of enjoying it.

Glossary

Additives   Synthetic chemicals added to foods during processing, as flavouring, colouring, preservatives, emulsifiers, stabilisers, and so on. More than 3000 chemicals are currently used by food manufacturers.

Amino acids   Protein's building blocks. There are twenty, of which eight are called 'essential' because the body cannot synthesise them.

Bran   The protective outer coating of a whole grain, high in fibre.

Calorie   A unit of energy measurement. A Calorie is the amount of heat required to raise the temperature of 1 kg (1000 grams) of water 1 °C. The combustion of food in the body produces heat energy. 1 gram of protein burned in the body has a heat/energy value of 4 Calories; 1 gram of carbohydrate 4 Calories; 1 gram of fat 9 Calories. Average adult daily requirements are about 2–3000 Calories. (See *Joule*).

Carbohydrates   The chief source of body fuel, consisting of carbon, hydrogen, and oxygen, with the hydrogen and oxygen in the same proportion as water. The richest sources are plant foods, especially sugars and starches.

Carotene   A yellow-orange pigment richly present in some fruits and vegetables, which is converted into Vitamin A in the body.

Cholesterol   A white, waxy alcohol manufactured by the liver and present in saturated animal fats.

Compost   *Humus* made from anything once living – weeds, leaves, grass cuttings, animal and bird dung, fruit and vegetable peelings, tea leaves, egg shells, even paper.

'Diseases of civilisation'   Heart disease, cancer, diabetes, and other killers which have reached epidemic proportions in the twentieth century.

Fats Fats have the same constituents as carbohydrates – carbon, hydrogen, and oxygen – but they have less oxygen in proportion to the hydrogen present. In *saturated* fats each carbon atom combines with two hydrogen atoms, except for the terminal carbon atoms, producing a fat solid at room temperature. *Unsaturated* fats have only some of their atoms joined with hydrogen, and they tend to be soft or liquid at room temperature.

Fibre Non-digestible plant cellulose, providing food bulk in the intestines and promoting food movement and daily emptying of the bowels. Dietary fibre is low in refined foods and high in whole grains (particularly the bran), vegetables, and fruits.

Health foods Natural whole foods, unrefined and free from chemical *additives*. Health food and whole food shops are specialist suppliers of health foods.

Humus The living part of soil, made up of organic matter, such as plant residues and animal droppings, which bacteria process into food for plants.

Hydrogenation Process used to increase the storage life of some fatty foods. The effect, as in ordinary margarine, is to harden and to partially saturate the food.

Joule Gradually replacing the Calorie in use as the unit of energy. 1 Calorie = 4·2 kilojoules (kJ).

Mineral salts Inorganic salts in plant and animal foods, eaten as compounds. Plants absorb the minerals in soil through their roots. Animals eat the plants.

Muesli Swiss breakfast of mixed cereals, milk, fruits, and nuts. The original formula is credited to Dr Max Bircher-Benner (1867–1939).

Organic farming The organic method of growing food, using *compost* or *humus* and not using chemical fertilisers.

Pesticides Chemical sprays used to kill insects on cereals, fruits and vegetables. Their use has increased enormously since the end of World War II.

Proteins Compounds of simpler units called alpha amino acids. Proteins consist of carbon, hydrogen, oxygen, nitrogen, and sometimes also phosphorus, sulphur, iron, and iodine. They are essential for building and repairing tissues and also supply energy. They can be obtained from both animal and plant foods.

Refining   Food is refined to make the texture smoother, whiter, and to improve storage life. Vital nutrients are removed in the process, some of which are sometimes replaced synthetically.

Sugars, natural   Sugars naturally present in fruits, vegetables, milk, and other foods. Sucrose is found in green plants, glucose in some fruits and vegetables, maltose in starch, and so on.

Supplements   Foods, drinks, tablets, etc which fortify the diet with concentrations of certain nutrients.

Vegan   A vegetarian who excludes milk, cheese, eggs, and all dairy products from the diet, and sometimes honey.

Vegetarian   A person who excludes meat, fish and poultry from the diet, though not usually dairy products. A vegetarian who drinks milk is sometimes called a lacto-vegetarian, and one who includes both milk and eggs in the diet is called a lacto-ovo-vegetarian.

Vitamins   Substances present in small amounts in foods but essential for regulating the body's internal activities. A deficiency of any vitamin causes disease.

Bibliography

Adams, Ruth, and Murray, Frank, *All You Should Know About Health Foods*, Larchmount Books, New York, 1975.

Annual Report of the Massachusetts Board of Agriculture, 1875.

Bircher, Ruth, *Eating Your Way to Health*, Faber and Faber, 1961.

Carson, Rachel, *The Sea Around Us*, Oxford University Press, New York, 1951; Staples Press, 1951.

Clark, Linda, *How to Improve Your Health: the Wholistic Approach*, Keats Publishing Inc., New Canaan, Connecticut, 1979.

Cleave, T., MD, *The Saccharine Disease*, Keats Publishing Inc., New Canaan, Connecticut, 1975.

Cleave, T. L., MD, Campbell, G. D., MD, and Painter, N. S., MD, *Coronary Thrombosis, Diabetes, and the Saccharine Disease*, John Wright and Sons, 1969.

Crawford, Michael A., MD, and Sheilagh, *What We Eat Today*, Neville Spearman, 1972.

Davis, Adelle, *Let's Get Well*, Harcourt, Brace and Jovanovich, New York, 1965; Allen and Unwin, 1966.

Day, Harvey, *Whole Foods For Health*, Thorsons, 1968.

Dixon, Pamela, *Ginseng*, Duckworth, 1976.

Elliot, Rose, *The Bean Book*, Collins, 1979.

Fredericks, Carlton, *Eating Right For You*, Grosset and Dunlap Inc., New York, 1972; Allen and Unwin, 1974.

Galton, Lawrence, *The Truth About Fibre in Your Diet*, Crown Publishers Inc., New York, 1976.

Gelb, Barbara Levine, *The Dictionary of Food and What's In It For You*, Paddington Press, 1978.

Hanssen, Maurice, *The Healing Power of Pollen*, Thorsons, 1979.

Hardy, Serena, *The Tea Book*, Whittet Books, 1979.

Hatfield, Audrey Wynne, *A Herb for Every Ill*, Dent, 1973.

Heaton, Kenneth W., MD, Preface to Jeanne Jones, *Fabulous Fibre Cookbook*, Pitman Books, 1978.

Hewitt, James, *New Faces*, A. Thomas, 1977.

Jarvis, D. C., MD, *Folk Medicine*, Henry Holt Inc., New York, 1958; W. H. Allen, 1960.

Knight, Margaret, *Teaching Nutrition and Food Science*, B. T. Batsford, 1976.

Kordel, Lelord, *Natural Folk Remedies*, Putnam's, New York, 1974; W. H. Allen, 1975.

Lane, Sir Arbuthnot, *The Prevention of Diseases Peculiar to Civilisation.*

Lappé, Frances Moore, *Diet for a Small Planet*, Ballentine Books, 1971. Revised edition 1975.

Law, Carl Edgar, 'Yes, Virginia, Drinking is Good For Your Health', *Macleans*, 11 February 1980.

Leyel, Mrs C. F., *The Truth About Herbs*, Culpeper Press, 1954.

Liddell, Caroline, *The Wholefoods Cookbook*, Coronet Books, Hodder and Stoughton, 1980.

Lucas, Jack, *Our Polluted Food: a Survey of the Risks*, Knight, 1975.

Manual of Nutrition, H.M.S.O. for the Ministry of Agriculture, Fisheries and Food, second edition, 1970.

Marno, Hazel, *Brown Baking*, Soil Association, Stowmarket, Suffolk.

Marshall, Anne, *The Pure Healthfood Cookbook*, Octopus Books, 1973.

McCance, R., and Widdowson, E., *The Composition of Foods*, H.M.S.O.

Nutrition Search, Inc., *Nutrition Almanac*, McGraw-Hill, New York, 1975.

Painter, Neill, MD, *The Lancet*, 30 June 1973.

Payler, D. K., MD, *The Lancet*, 16 June 1973.

Percival, Lloyd, *American Bee Journal*, Hamilton, Illinois, October 1955.

Platt, Rutherford, *The Great American Forest*, Prentice-Hall Inc., New York, 1965.

Rodale, J. I., *Health Treasury*, Rodale Press Inc., 1962.

Rorty, James and Norman, N. P., MD, *Bio-organics: Your Food and Your Health*, Devin-Adair Co., Connecticut, 1956.

Seddon, George and Burrow, Jackie, *The Wholefood Book*, Mitchell Beazley, 1978.

Sekules, Veronica, *Friends of the Earth Cookbook*, Penguin, 1980.

Shute, Wilfrid, MD, *Complete Updated Vitamin E Book*, Keats Publishing Inc., New Canaan, Connecticut, 1975.

Wade, Carlson, *Fact Book on Fats, Oils, and Cholesterol*, Keats Publishing Inc., New Canaan, Connecticut, 1973.

Watts, B. K. and Merrill, A. L., *Composition of Foods*, US Department of Agriculture, 1963.

Williams, Roger J., MD, *Nutrition Against Disease*, Pitman Books, New York, 1971.

Wood, H. Curtis, Jr, MD, *Overfed and Undernourished*, Exposition Press, 1959; as *Calories, Vitamins and Common Sense*, Belmont Books, New York, 1962.

Wordsworth, Jill, *Diet Revolution Food Reform: Your Questions Answered*, Victor Gollancz, 1976.

Wynne-Tyson, Jon, *Food For a Future: the Ecological Priority Of a Humane Diet*, Davis-Poynter Ltd., 1975; Centaur Press Ltd., 1979.

Yudkin, John, *Nutrition*, Teach Yourself Books, Hodder and Stoughton, 1977.

Yudkin, John, *This Slimming Business*, MacGibbon and Kee Ltd., 1958; Penguin, 1962.

Index